ADHD Planner

INFORMATION

NAME

ADDRESS

E-MAIL ADDRESS

WEBSITE

PHONE   **FAX**

EMERGENCY CONTACT PERSON

PHONE   **FAX**

DAY GOALS

1 ....
2 ....
3 ....

DATE
WEEK
LOCATION
WEIGHT

Mood Tracker

BEHAVIOR

INATTENTION

SHORT ATTENTION	① ② ③ ④ ⑤ ⑥ ⑦ ⑧ ⑨ ⑩
UNMOTIVATED / BORED	① ② ③ ④ ⑤ ⑥ ⑦ ⑧ ⑨ ⑩
SHORT ATTENTION	① ② ③ ④ ⑤ ⑥ ⑦ ⑧ ⑨ ⑩
FORGETFUL / CONFUSIONED	① ② ③ ④ ⑤ ⑥ ⑦ ⑧ ⑨ ⑩

HYPERACTIVITY

CONSTANTLY MOVING / TALKING	① ② ③ ④ ⑤ ⑥ ⑦ ⑧ ⑨ ⑩
STRUGGLING TO SIT STILL	① ② ③ ④ ⑤ ⑥ ⑦ ⑧ ⑨ ⑩
TOUCHING THINGS REPEATEDLY	① ② ③ ④ ⑤ ⑥ ⑦ ⑧ ⑨ ⑩
DIFFICULT SLEEPING	① ② ③ ④ ⑤ ⑥ ⑦ ⑧ ⑨ ⑩

IMPULSIVITY

ACTING WITHOUT THINKING	① ② ③ ④ ⑤ ⑥ ⑦ ⑧ ⑨ ⑩
INTERRUPTING OTHERS	① ② ③ ④ ⑤ ⑥ ⑦ ⑧ ⑨ ⑩
EASILY FRUSTRATED	① ② ③ ④ ⑤ ⑥ ⑦ ⑧ ⑨ ⑩
UNABLE TO HOLD BACK EMOTIONS	① ② ③ ④ ⑤ ⑥ ⑦ ⑧ ⑨ ⑩

MEALS

MEDICATIONS

Water Tracker

NOTES

....
....

1 ....
2 ....
3 ....

DATE
WEEK
LOCATION
WEIGHT

Mood Tracker

BEHAVIOR

INATTENTION

SHORT ATTENTION	① ② ③ ④ ⑤ ⑥ ⑦ ⑧ ⑨ ⑩
UNMOTIVATED / BORED	① ② ③ ④ ⑤ ⑥ ⑦ ⑧ ⑨ ⑩
SHORT ATTENTION	① ② ③ ④ ⑤ ⑥ ⑦ ⑧ ⑨ ⑩
FORGETFUL / CONFUSIONED	① ② ③ ④ ⑤ ⑥ ⑦ ⑧ ⑨ ⑩

HYPERACTIVITY

CONSTANTLY MOVING / TALKING	① ② ③ ④ ⑤ ⑥ ⑦ ⑧ ⑨ ⑩
STRUGGLING TO SIT STILL	① ② ③ ④ ⑤ ⑥ ⑦ ⑧ ⑨ ⑩
TOUCHING THINGS REPEATEDLY	① ② ③ ④ ⑤ ⑥ ⑦ ⑧ ⑨ ⑩
DIFFICULT SLEEPING	① ② ③ ④ ⑤ ⑥ ⑦ ⑧ ⑨ ⑩

IMPULSIVITY

ACTING WITHOUT THINKING	① ② ③ ④ ⑤ ⑥ ⑦ ⑧ ⑨ ⑩
INTERRUPTING OTHERS	① ② ③ ④ ⑤ ⑥ ⑦ ⑧ ⑨ ⑩
EASILY FRUSTRATED	① ② ③ ④ ⑤ ⑥ ⑦ ⑧ ⑨ ⑩
UNABLE TO HOLD BACK EMOTIONS	① ② ③ ④ ⑤ ⑥ ⑦ ⑧ ⑨ ⑩

MEALS

MEDICATIONS

Water Tracker

NOTES

....
....

<table>
<tr><td>

DAY GOALS

1 ....
2 ....
3 ....

</td><td>

DATE

WEEK

LOCATION

WEIGHT

</td></tr>
</table>

Mood Tracker

BEHAVIOR

INATTENTION

SHORT ATTENTION	① ② ③ ④ ⑤ ⑥ ⑦ ⑧ ⑨ ⑩
UNMOTIVATED / BORED	① ② ③ ④ ⑤ ⑥ ⑦ ⑧ ⑨ ⑩
SHORT ATTENTION	① ② ③ ④ ⑤ ⑥ ⑦ ⑧ ⑨ ⑩
FORGETFUL / CONFUSIONED	① ② ③ ④ ⑤ ⑥ ⑦ ⑧ ⑨ ⑩

HYPERACTIVITY

CONSTANTLY MOVING / TALKING	① ② ③ ④ ⑤ ⑥ ⑦ ⑧ ⑨ ⑩
STRUGGLING TO SIT STILL	① ② ③ ④ ⑤ ⑥ ⑦ ⑧ ⑨ ⑩
TOUCHING THINGS REPEATEDLY	① ② ③ ④ ⑤ ⑥ ⑦ ⑧ ⑨ ⑩
DIFFICULT SLEEPING	① ② ③ ④ ⑤ ⑥ ⑦ ⑧ ⑨ ⑩

IMPULSIVITY

ACTING WITHOUT THINKING	① ② ③ ④ ⑤ ⑥ ⑦ ⑧ ⑨ ⑩
INTERRUPTING OTHERS	① ② ③ ④ ⑤ ⑥ ⑦ ⑧ ⑨ ⑩
EASILY FRUSTRATED	① ② ③ ④ ⑤ ⑥ ⑦ ⑧ ⑨ ⑩
UNABLE TO HOLD BACK EMOTIONS	① ② ③ ④ ⑤ ⑥ ⑦ ⑧ ⑨ ⑩

MEALS	MEDICATIONS

Water Tracker

NOTES

....
....

<table>
<tr><td>

DAY GOALS

1 ....
2 ....
3 ....

</td><td>

DATE

WEEK

LOCATION

WEIGHT

</td></tr>
</table>

Mood Tracker

BEHAVIOR

INATTENTION

SHORT ATTENTION	① ② ③ ④ ⑤ ⑥ ⑦ ⑧ ⑨ ⑩
UNMOTIVATED / BORED	① ② ③ ④ ⑤ ⑥ ⑦ ⑧ ⑨ ⑩
SHORT ATTENTION	① ② ③ ④ ⑤ ⑥ ⑦ ⑧ ⑨ ⑩
FORGETFUL / CONFUSIONED	① ② ③ ④ ⑤ ⑥ ⑦ ⑧ ⑨ ⑩

HYPERACTIVITY

CONSTANTLY MOVING / TALKING	① ② ③ ④ ⑤ ⑥ ⑦ ⑧ ⑨ ⑩
STRUGGLING TO SIT STILL	① ② ③ ④ ⑤ ⑥ ⑦ ⑧ ⑨ ⑩
TOUCHING THINGS REPEATEDLY	① ② ③ ④ ⑤ ⑥ ⑦ ⑧ ⑨ ⑩
DIFFICULT SLEEPING	① ② ③ ④ ⑤ ⑥ ⑦ ⑧ ⑨ ⑩

IMPULSIVITY

ACTING WITHOUT THINKING	① ② ③ ④ ⑤ ⑥ ⑦ ⑧ ⑨ ⑩
INTERRUPTING OTHERS	① ② ③ ④ ⑤ ⑥ ⑦ ⑧ ⑨ ⑩
EASILY FRUSTRATED	① ② ③ ④ ⑤ ⑥ ⑦ ⑧ ⑨ ⑩
UNABLE TO HOLD BACK EMOTIONS	① ② ③ ④ ⑤ ⑥ ⑦ ⑧ ⑨ ⑩

MEALS

MEDICATIONS

Water Tracker

NOTES

....
....

<table>
<tr><td>

DAY GOALS

1 ....
2 ....
3 ....

</td><td>

DATE

WEEK

LOCATION

WEIGHT

</td></tr>
</table>

Mood Tracker

BEHAVIOR

INATTENTION

SHORT ATTENTION	① ② ③ ④ ⑤ ⑥ ⑦ ⑧ ⑨ ⑩
UNMOTIVATED / BORED	① ② ③ ④ ⑤ ⑥ ⑦ ⑧ ⑨ ⑩
SHORT ATTENTION	① ② ③ ④ ⑤ ⑥ ⑦ ⑧ ⑨ ⑩
FORGETFUL / CONFUSIONED	① ② ③ ④ ⑤ ⑥ ⑦ ⑧ ⑨ ⑩

HYPERACTIVITY

CONSTANTLY MOVING / TALKING	① ② ③ ④ ⑤ ⑥ ⑦ ⑧ ⑨ ⑩
STRUGGLING TO SIT STILL	① ② ③ ④ ⑤ ⑥ ⑦ ⑧ ⑨ ⑩
TOUCHING THINGS REPEATEDLY	① ② ③ ④ ⑤ ⑥ ⑦ ⑧ ⑨ ⑩
DIFFICULT SLEEPING	① ② ③ ④ ⑤ ⑥ ⑦ ⑧ ⑨ ⑩

IMPULSIVITY

ACTING WITHOUT THINKING	① ② ③ ④ ⑤ ⑥ ⑦ ⑧ ⑨ ⑩
INTERRUPTING OTHERS	① ② ③ ④ ⑤ ⑥ ⑦ ⑧ ⑨ ⑩
EASILY FRUSTRATED	① ② ③ ④ ⑤ ⑥ ⑦ ⑧ ⑨ ⑩
UNABLE TO HOLD BACK EMOTIONS	① ② ③ ④ ⑤ ⑥ ⑦ ⑧ ⑨ ⑩

MEALS

MEDICATIONS

Water Tracker

NOTES

....
....

DAY GOALS

1 ....
2 ....
3 ....

DATE

WEEK

LOCATION

WEIGHT

Mood Tracker

BEHAVIOR

INATTENTION

SHORT ATTENTION	① ② ③ ④ ⑤ ⑥ ⑦ ⑧ ⑨ ⑩
UNMOTIVATED / BORED	① ② ③ ④ ⑤ ⑥ ⑦ ⑧ ⑨ ⑩
SHORT ATTENTION	① ② ③ ④ ⑤ ⑥ ⑦ ⑧ ⑨ ⑩
FORGETFUL / CONFUSIONED	① ② ③ ④ ⑤ ⑥ ⑦ ⑧ ⑨ ⑩

HYPERACTIVITY

CONSTANTLY MOVING / TALKING	① ② ③ ④ ⑤ ⑥ ⑦ ⑧ ⑨ ⑩
STRUGGLING TO SIT STILL	① ② ③ ④ ⑤ ⑥ ⑦ ⑧ ⑨ ⑩
TOUCHING THINGS REPEATEDLY	① ② ③ ④ ⑤ ⑥ ⑦ ⑧ ⑨ ⑩
DIFFICULT SLEEPING	① ② ③ ④ ⑤ ⑥ ⑦ ⑧ ⑨ ⑩

IMPULSIVITY

ACTING WITHOUT THINKING	① ② ③ ④ ⑤ ⑥ ⑦ ⑧ ⑨ ⑩
INTERRUPTING OTHERS	① ② ③ ④ ⑤ ⑥ ⑦ ⑧ ⑨ ⑩
EASILY FRUSTRATED	① ② ③ ④ ⑤ ⑥ ⑦ ⑧ ⑨ ⑩
UNABLE TO HOLD BACK EMOTIONS	① ② ③ ④ ⑤ ⑥ ⑦ ⑧ ⑨ ⑩

MEALS

MEDICATIONS

Water Tracker

NOTES

....
....

1 ....
2 ....
3 ....

DATE
WEEK
LOCATION
WEIGHT

Mood Tracker

BEHAVIOR

INATTENTION

SHORT ATTENTION ① ② ③ ④ ⑤ ⑥ ⑦ ⑧ ⑨ ⑩
UNMOTIVATED / BORED ① ② ③ ④ ⑤ ⑥ ⑦ ⑧ ⑨ ⑩
SHORT ATTENTION ① ② ③ ④ ⑤ ⑥ ⑦ ⑧ ⑨ ⑩
FORGETFUL / CONFUSIONED ① ② ③ ④ ⑤ ⑥ ⑦ ⑧ ⑨ ⑩

HYPERACTIVITY

CONSTANTLY MOVING / TALKING ① ② ③ ④ ⑤ ⑥ ⑦ ⑧ ⑨ ⑩
STRUGGLING TO SIT STILL ① ② ③ ④ ⑤ ⑥ ⑦ ⑧ ⑨ ⑩
TOUCHING THINGS REPEATEDLY ① ② ③ ④ ⑤ ⑥ ⑦ ⑧ ⑨ ⑩
DIFFICULT SLEEPING ① ② ③ ④ ⑤ ⑥ ⑦ ⑧ ⑨ ⑩

IMPULSIVITY

ACTING WITHOUT THINKING ① ② ③ ④ ⑤ ⑥ ⑦ ⑧ ⑨ ⑩
INTERRUPTING OTHERS ① ② ③ ④ ⑤ ⑥ ⑦ ⑧ ⑨ ⑩
EASILY FRUSTRATED ① ② ③ ④ ⑤ ⑥ ⑦ ⑧ ⑨ ⑩
UNABLE TO HOLD BACK EMOTIONS ① ② ③ ④ ⑤ ⑥ ⑦ ⑧ ⑨ ⑩

MEALS

MEDICATIONS

Water Tracker

NOTES

....
....

<table>
<tr><td>

DAY GOALS

1 ....
2 ....
3 ....

</td><td>

DATE

WEEK

LOCATION

WEIGHT

</td></tr>
</table>

Mood Tracker

BEHAVIOR

INATTENTION

SHORT ATTENTION	① ② ③ ④ ⑤ ⑥ ⑦ ⑧ ⑨ ⑩
UNMOTIVATED / BORED	① ② ③ ④ ⑤ ⑥ ⑦ ⑧ ⑨ ⑩
SHORT ATTENTION	① ② ③ ④ ⑤ ⑥ ⑦ ⑧ ⑨ ⑩
FORGETFUL / CONFUSIONED	① ② ③ ④ ⑤ ⑥ ⑦ ⑧ ⑨ ⑩

HYPERACTIVITY

CONSTANTLY MOVING / TALKING	① ② ③ ④ ⑤ ⑥ ⑦ ⑧ ⑨ ⑩
STRUGGLING TO SIT STILL	① ② ③ ④ ⑤ ⑥ ⑦ ⑧ ⑨ ⑩
TOUCHING THINGS REPEATEDLY	① ② ③ ④ ⑤ ⑥ ⑦ ⑧ ⑨ ⑩
DIFFICULT SLEEPING	① ② ③ ④ ⑤ ⑥ ⑦ ⑧ ⑨ ⑩

IMPULSIVITY

ACTING WITHOUT THINKING	① ② ③ ④ ⑤ ⑥ ⑦ ⑧ ⑨ ⑩
INTERRUPTING OTHERS	① ② ③ ④ ⑤ ⑥ ⑦ ⑧ ⑨ ⑩
EASILY FRUSTRATED	① ② ③ ④ ⑤ ⑥ ⑦ ⑧ ⑨ ⑩
UNABLE TO HOLD BACK EMOTIONS	① ② ③ ④ ⑤ ⑥ ⑦ ⑧ ⑨ ⑩

MEALS

MEDICATIONS

Water Tracker

NOTES

....

....

<table>
<tr><td>

DAY GOALS

1 ....
2 ....
3 ....

</td><td>

DATE

WEEK

LOCATION

WEIGHT

</td></tr>
</table>

Mood Tracker

BEHAVIOR

INATTENTION

SHORT ATTENTION	① ② ③ ④ ⑤ ⑥ ⑦ ⑧ ⑨ ⑩
UNMOTIVATED / BORED	① ② ③ ④ ⑤ ⑥ ⑦ ⑧ ⑨ ⑩
SHORT ATTENTION	① ② ③ ④ ⑤ ⑥ ⑦ ⑧ ⑨ ⑩
FORGETFUL / CONFUSIONED	① ② ③ ④ ⑤ ⑥ ⑦ ⑧ ⑨ ⑩

HYPERACTIVITY

CONSTANTLY MOVING / TALKING	① ② ③ ④ ⑤ ⑥ ⑦ ⑧ ⑨ ⑩
STRUGGLING TO SIT STILL	① ② ③ ④ ⑤ ⑥ ⑦ ⑧ ⑨ ⑩
TOUCHING THINGS REPEATEDLY	① ② ③ ④ ⑤ ⑥ ⑦ ⑧ ⑨ ⑩
DIFFICULT SLEEPING	① ② ③ ④ ⑤ ⑥ ⑦ ⑧ ⑨ ⑩

IMPULSIVITY

ACTING WITHOUT THINKING	① ② ③ ④ ⑤ ⑥ ⑦ ⑧ ⑨ ⑩
INTERRUPTING OTHERS	① ② ③ ④ ⑤ ⑥ ⑦ ⑧ ⑨ ⑩
EASILY FRUSTRATED	① ② ③ ④ ⑤ ⑥ ⑦ ⑧ ⑨ ⑩
UNABLE TO HOLD BACK EMOTIONS	① ② ③ ④ ⑤ ⑥ ⑦ ⑧ ⑨ ⑩

MEALS	MEDICATIONS

Water Tracker

NOTES

....
....

<table>
<tr><td>

DAY GOALS

1 ....
2 ....
3 ....

</td><td>

DATE

WEEK

LOCATION

WEIGHT

</td></tr>
</table>

Mood Tracker

BEHAVIOR

INATTENTION

SHORT ATTENTION	① ② ③ ④ ⑤ ⑥ ⑦ ⑧ ⑨ ⑩
UNMOTIVATED / BORED	① ② ③ ④ ⑤ ⑥ ⑦ ⑧ ⑨ ⑩
SHORT ATTENTION	① ② ③ ④ ⑤ ⑥ ⑦ ⑧ ⑨ ⑩
FORGETFUL / CONFUSIONED	① ② ③ ④ ⑤ ⑥ ⑦ ⑧ ⑨ ⑩

HYPERACTIVITY

CONSTANTLY MOVING / TALKING	① ② ③ ④ ⑤ ⑥ ⑦ ⑧ ⑨ ⑩
STRUGGLING TO SIT STILL	① ② ③ ④ ⑤ ⑥ ⑦ ⑧ ⑨ ⑩
TOUCHING THINGS REPEATEDLY	① ② ③ ④ ⑤ ⑥ ⑦ ⑧ ⑨ ⑩
DIFFICULT SLEEPING	① ② ③ ④ ⑤ ⑥ ⑦ ⑧ ⑨ ⑩

IMPULSIVITY

ACTING WITHOUT THINKING	① ② ③ ④ ⑤ ⑥ ⑦ ⑧ ⑨ ⑩
INTERRUPTING OTHERS	① ② ③ ④ ⑤ ⑥ ⑦ ⑧ ⑨ ⑩
EASILY FRUSTRATED	① ② ③ ④ ⑤ ⑥ ⑦ ⑧ ⑨ ⑩
UNABLE TO HOLD BACK EMOTIONS	① ② ③ ④ ⑤ ⑥ ⑦ ⑧ ⑨ ⑩

MEALS

MEDICATIONS

Water Tracker

NOTES

....
....

Mood Tracker

BEHAVIOR

INATTENTION

SHORT ATTENTION	① ② ③ ④ ⑤ ⑥ ⑦ ⑧ ⑨ ⑩
UNMOTIVATED / BORED	① ② ③ ④ ⑤ ⑥ ⑦ ⑧ ⑨ ⑩
SHORT ATTENTION	① ② ③ ④ ⑤ ⑥ ⑦ ⑧ ⑨ ⑩
FORGETFUL / CONFUSIONED	① ② ③ ④ ⑤ ⑥ ⑦ ⑧ ⑨ ⑩

HYPERACTIVITY

CONSTANTLY MOVING / TALKING	① ② ③ ④ ⑤ ⑥ ⑦ ⑧ ⑨ ⑩
STRUGGLING TO SIT STILL	① ② ③ ④ ⑤ ⑥ ⑦ ⑧ ⑨ ⑩
TOUCHING THINGS REPEATEDLY	① ② ③ ④ ⑤ ⑥ ⑦ ⑧ ⑨ ⑩
DIFFICULT SLEEPING	① ② ③ ④ ⑤ ⑥ ⑦ ⑧ ⑨ ⑩

IMPULSIVITY

ACTING WITHOUT THINKING	① ② ③ ④ ⑤ ⑥ ⑦ ⑧ ⑨ ⑩
INTERRUPTING OTHERS	① ② ③ ④ ⑤ ⑥ ⑦ ⑧ ⑨ ⑩
EASILY FRUSTRATED	① ② ③ ④ ⑤ ⑥ ⑦ ⑧ ⑨ ⑩
UNABLE TO HOLD BACK EMOTIONS	① ② ③ ④ ⑤ ⑥ ⑦ ⑧ ⑨ ⑩

MEALS

MEDICATIONS

Water Tracker

NOTES

....
....

<table>
<tr><td>

DAY GOALS

1 ....
2 ....
3 ....

</td><td>

DATE

WEEK

LOCATION

WEIGHT

</td></tr>
</table>

Mood Tracker

BEHAVIOR

INATTENTION

SHORT ATTENTION	① ② ③ ④ ⑤ ⑥ ⑦ ⑧ ⑨ ⑩
UNMOTIVATED / BORED	① ② ③ ④ ⑤ ⑥ ⑦ ⑧ ⑨ ⑩
SHORT ATTENTION	① ② ③ ④ ⑤ ⑥ ⑦ ⑧ ⑨ ⑩
FORGETFUL / CONFUSIONED	① ② ③ ④ ⑤ ⑥ ⑦ ⑧ ⑨ ⑩

HYPERACTIVITY

CONSTANTLY MOVING / TALKING	① ② ③ ④ ⑤ ⑥ ⑦ ⑧ ⑨ ⑩
STRUGGLING TO SIT STILL	① ② ③ ④ ⑤ ⑥ ⑦ ⑧ ⑨ ⑩
TOUCHING THINGS REPEATEDLY	① ② ③ ④ ⑤ ⑥ ⑦ ⑧ ⑨ ⑩
DIFFICULT SLEEPING	① ② ③ ④ ⑤ ⑥ ⑦ ⑧ ⑨ ⑩

IMPULSIVITY

ACTING WITHOUT THINKING	① ② ③ ④ ⑤ ⑥ ⑦ ⑧ ⑨ ⑩
INTERRUPTING OTHERS	① ② ③ ④ ⑤ ⑥ ⑦ ⑧ ⑨ ⑩
EASILY FRUSTRATED	① ② ③ ④ ⑤ ⑥ ⑦ ⑧ ⑨ ⑩
UNABLE TO HOLD BACK EMOTIONS	① ② ③ ④ ⑤ ⑥ ⑦ ⑧ ⑨ ⑩

MEALS	MEDICATIONS

Water Tracker

NOTES

....
....

<table>
<tr><td>

DAY GOALS

1 ....
2 ....
3 ....

</td><td>

DATE

WEEK

LOCATION

WEIGHT

</td></tr>
</table>

Mood Tracker

BEHAVIOR

INATTENTION

SHORT ATTENTION	① ② ③ ④ ⑤ ⑥ ⑦ ⑧ ⑨ ⑩
UNMOTIVATED / BORED	① ② ③ ④ ⑤ ⑥ ⑦ ⑧ ⑨ ⑩
SHORT ATTENTION	① ② ③ ④ ⑤ ⑥ ⑦ ⑧ ⑨ ⑩
FORGETFUL / CONFUSIONED	① ② ③ ④ ⑤ ⑥ ⑦ ⑧ ⑨ ⑩

HYPERACTIVITY

CONSTANTLY MOVING / TALKING	① ② ③ ④ ⑤ ⑥ ⑦ ⑧ ⑨ ⑩
STRUGGLING TO SIT STILL	① ② ③ ④ ⑤ ⑥ ⑦ ⑧ ⑨ ⑩
TOUCHING THINGS REPEATEDLY	① ② ③ ④ ⑤ ⑥ ⑦ ⑧ ⑨ ⑩
DIFFICULT SLEEPING	① ② ③ ④ ⑤ ⑥ ⑦ ⑧ ⑨ ⑩

IMPULSIVITY

ACTING WITHOUT THINKING	① ② ③ ④ ⑤ ⑥ ⑦ ⑧ ⑨ ⑩
INTERRUPTING OTHERS	① ② ③ ④ ⑤ ⑥ ⑦ ⑧ ⑨ ⑩
EASILY FRUSTRATED	① ② ③ ④ ⑤ ⑥ ⑦ ⑧ ⑨ ⑩
UNABLE TO HOLD BACK EMOTIONS	① ② ③ ④ ⑤ ⑥ ⑦ ⑧ ⑨ ⑩

MEALS

MEDICATIONS

Water Tracker

NOTES

....
....

Mood Tracker

BEHAVIOR

INATTENTION

SHORT ATTENTION	1 2 3 4 5 6 7 8 9 10
UNMOTIVATED / BORED	1 2 3 4 5 6 7 8 9 10
SHORT ATTENTION	1 2 3 4 5 6 7 8 9 10
FORGETFUL / CONFUSIONED	1 2 3 4 5 6 7 8 9 10

HYPERACTIVITY

CONSTANTLY MOVING / TALKING	1 2 3 4 5 6 7 8 9 10
STRUGGLING TO SIT STILL	1 2 3 4 5 6 7 8 9 10
TOUCHING THINGS REPEATEDLY	1 2 3 4 5 6 7 8 9 10
DIFFICULT SLEEPING	1 2 3 4 5 6 7 8 9 10

IMPULSIVITY

ACTING WITHOUT THINKING	1 2 3 4 5 6 7 8 9 10
INTERRUPTING OTHERS	1 2 3 4 5 6 7 8 9 10
EASILY FRUSTRATED	1 2 3 4 5 6 7 8 9 10
UNABLE TO HOLD BACK EMOTIONS	1 2 3 4 5 6 7 8 9 10

MEALS

MEDICATIONS

Water Tracker

NOTES

DAY GOALS

1 ....
2 ....
3 ....

DATE

WEEK

LOCATION

WEIGHT

Mood Tracker

BEHAVIOR

INATTENTION

SHORT ATTENTION	① ② ③ ④ ⑤ ⑥ ⑦ ⑧ ⑨ ⑩
UNMOTIVATED / BORED	① ② ③ ④ ⑤ ⑥ ⑦ ⑧ ⑨ ⑩
SHORT ATTENTION	① ② ③ ④ ⑤ ⑥ ⑦ ⑧ ⑨ ⑩
FORGETFUL / CONFUSIONED	① ② ③ ④ ⑤ ⑥ ⑦ ⑧ ⑨ ⑩

HYPERACTIVITY

CONSTANTLY MOVING / TALKING	① ② ③ ④ ⑤ ⑥ ⑦ ⑧ ⑨ ⑩
STRUGGLING TO SIT STILL	① ② ③ ④ ⑤ ⑥ ⑦ ⑧ ⑨ ⑩
TOUCHING THINGS REPEATEDLY	① ② ③ ④ ⑤ ⑥ ⑦ ⑧ ⑨ ⑩
DIFFICULT SLEEPING	① ② ③ ④ ⑤ ⑥ ⑦ ⑧ ⑨ ⑩

IMPULSIVITY

ACTING WITHOUT THINKING	① ② ③ ④ ⑤ ⑥ ⑦ ⑧ ⑨ ⑩
INTERRUPTING OTHERS	① ② ③ ④ ⑤ ⑥ ⑦ ⑧ ⑨ ⑩
EASILY FRUSTRATED	① ② ③ ④ ⑤ ⑥ ⑦ ⑧ ⑨ ⑩
UNABLE TO HOLD BACK EMOTIONS	① ② ③ ④ ⑤ ⑥ ⑦ ⑧ ⑨ ⑩

MEALS

MEDICATIONS

Water Tracker

NOTES

....
....

1 ....
2 ....
3 ....

DATE
WEEK
LOCATION
WEIGHT

Mood Tracker

BEHAVIOR

INATTENTION

SHORT ATTENTION	1 2 3 4 5 6 7 8 9 10
UNMOTIVATED / BORED	1 2 3 4 5 6 7 8 9 10
SHORT ATTENTION	1 2 3 4 5 6 7 8 9 10
FORGETFUL / CONFUSIONED	1 2 3 4 5 6 7 8 9 10

HYPERACTIVITY

CONSTANTLY MOVING / TALKING	1 2 3 4 5 6 7 8 9 10
STRUGGLING TO SIT STILL	1 2 3 4 5 6 7 8 9 10
TOUCHING THINGS REPEATEDLY	1 2 3 4 5 6 7 8 9 10
DIFFICULT SLEEPING	1 2 3 4 5 6 7 8 9 10

IMPULSIVITY

ACTING WITHOUT THINKING	1 2 3 4 5 6 7 8 9 10
INTERRUPTING OTHERS	1 2 3 4 5 6 7 8 9 10
EASILY FRUSTRATED	1 2 3 4 5 6 7 8 9 10
UNABLE TO HOLD BACK EMOTIONS	1 2 3 4 5 6 7 8 9 10

MEALS

MEDICATIONS

Water Tracker

NOTES

....
....

Mood Tracker

INATTENTION

SHORT ATTENTION	1 2 3 4 5 6 7 8 9 10
UNMOTIVATED / BORED	1 2 3 4 5 6 7 8 9 10
SHORT ATTENTION	1 2 3 4 5 6 7 8 9 10
FORGETFUL / CONFUSIONED	1 2 3 4 5 6 7 8 9 10

HYPERACTIVITY

CONSTANTLY MOVING / TALKING	1 2 3 4 5 6 7 8 9 10
STRUGGLING TO SIT STILL	1 2 3 4 5 6 7 8 9 10
TOUCHING THINGS REPEATEDLY	1 2 3 4 5 6 7 8 9 10
DIFFICULT SLEEPING	1 2 3 4 5 6 7 8 9 10

IMPULSIVITY

ACTING WITHOUT THINKING	1 2 3 4 5 6 7 8 9 10
INTERRUPTING OTHERS	1 2 3 4 5 6 7 8 9 10
EASILY FRUSTRATED	1 2 3 4 5 6 7 8 9 10
UNABLE TO HOLD BACK EMOTIONS	1 2 3 4 5 6 7 8 9 10

MEALS

MEDICATIONS

Water Tracker

NOTES

DATE

WEEK

LOCATION

WEIGHT

Mood Tracker

BEHAVIOR

INATTENTION

SHORT ATTENTION	1 2 3 4 5 6 7 8 9 10
UNMOTIVATED / BORED	1 2 3 4 5 6 7 8 9 10
SHORT ATTENTION	1 2 3 4 5 6 7 8 9 10
FORGETFUL / CONFUSIONED	1 2 3 4 5 6 7 8 9 10

HYPERACTIVITY

CONSTANTLY MOVING / TALKING	1 2 3 4 5 6 7 8 9 10
STRUGGLING TO SIT STILL	1 2 3 4 5 6 7 8 9 10
TOUCHING THINGS REPEATEDLY	1 2 3 4 5 6 7 8 9 10
DIFFICULT SLEEPING	1 2 3 4 5 6 7 8 9 10

IMPULSIVITY

ACTING WITHOUT THINKING	1 2 3 4 5 6 7 8 9 10
INTERRUPTING OTHERS	1 2 3 4 5 6 7 8 9 10
EASILY FRUSTRATED	1 2 3 4 5 6 7 8 9 10
UNABLE TO HOLD BACK EMOTIONS	1 2 3 4 5 6 7 8 9 10

MEALS

MEDICATIONS

Water Tracker

NOTES

<table>
<tr><td>

DAY GOALS

1 ....
2 ....
3 ....

</td><td>

DATE

WEEK

LOCATION

WEIGHT

</td></tr>
</table>

Mood Tracker

BEHAVIOR

INATTENTION

SHORT ATTENTION	1 2 3 4 5 6 7 8 9 10
UNMOTIVATED / BORED	1 2 3 4 5 6 7 8 9 10
SHORT ATTENTION	1 2 3 4 5 6 7 8 9 10
FORGETFUL / CONFUSIONED	1 2 3 4 5 6 7 8 9 10

HYPERACTIVITY

CONSTANTLY MOVING / TALKING	1 2 3 4 5 6 7 8 9 10
STRUGGLING TO SIT STILL	1 2 3 4 5 6 7 8 9 10
TOUCHING THINGS REPEATEDLY	1 2 3 4 5 6 7 8 9 10
DIFFICULT SLEEPING	1 2 3 4 5 6 7 8 9 10

IMPULSIVITY

ACTING WITHOUT THINKING	1 2 3 4 5 6 7 8 9 10
INTERRUPTING OTHERS	1 2 3 4 5 6 7 8 9 10
EASILY FRUSTRATED	1 2 3 4 5 6 7 8 9 10
UNABLE TO HOLD BACK EMOTIONS	1 2 3 4 5 6 7 8 9 10

MEALS

MEDICATIONS

Water Tracker

NOTES

....
....

Mood Tracker

BEHAVIOR

INATTENTION

SHORT ATTENTION	① ② ③ ④ ⑤ ⑥ ⑦ ⑧ ⑨ ⑩
UNMOTIVATED / BORED	① ② ③ ④ ⑤ ⑥ ⑦ ⑧ ⑨ ⑩
SHORT ATTENTION	① ② ③ ④ ⑤ ⑥ ⑦ ⑧ ⑨ ⑩
FORGETFUL / CONFUSIONED	① ② ③ ④ ⑤ ⑥ ⑦ ⑧ ⑨ ⑩

HYPERACTIVITY

CONSTANTLY MOVING / TALKING	① ② ③ ④ ⑤ ⑥ ⑦ ⑧ ⑨ ⑩
STRUGGLING TO SIT STILL	① ② ③ ④ ⑤ ⑥ ⑦ ⑧ ⑨ ⑩
TOUCHING THINGS REPEATEDLY	① ② ③ ④ ⑤ ⑥ ⑦ ⑧ ⑨ ⑩
DIFFICULT SLEEPING	① ② ③ ④ ⑤ ⑥ ⑦ ⑧ ⑨ ⑩

IMPULSIVITY

ACTING WITHOUT THINKING	① ② ③ ④ ⑤ ⑥ ⑦ ⑧ ⑨ ⑩
INTERRUPTING OTHERS	① ② ③ ④ ⑤ ⑥ ⑦ ⑧ ⑨ ⑩
EASILY FRUSTRATED	① ② ③ ④ ⑤ ⑥ ⑦ ⑧ ⑨ ⑩
UNABLE TO HOLD BACK EMOTIONS	① ② ③ ④ ⑤ ⑥ ⑦ ⑧ ⑨ ⑩

MEALS

MEDICATIONS

Water Tracker

NOTES

DATE

WEEK

LOCATION

WEIGHT

Mood Tracker

BEHAVIOR

INATTENTION

SHORT ATTENTION	① ② ③ ④ ⑤ ⑥ ⑦ ⑧ ⑨ ⑩
UNMOTIVATED / BORED	① ② ③ ④ ⑤ ⑥ ⑦ ⑧ ⑨ ⑩
SHORT ATTENTION	① ② ③ ④ ⑤ ⑥ ⑦ ⑧ ⑨ ⑩
FORGETFUL / CONFUSIONED	① ② ③ ④ ⑤ ⑥ ⑦ ⑧ ⑨ ⑩

HYPERACTIVITY

CONSTANTLY MOVING / TALKING	① ② ③ ④ ⑤ ⑥ ⑦ ⑧ ⑨ ⑩
STRUGGLING TO SIT STILL	① ② ③ ④ ⑤ ⑥ ⑦ ⑧ ⑨ ⑩
TOUCHING THINGS REPEATEDLY	① ② ③ ④ ⑤ ⑥ ⑦ ⑧ ⑨ ⑩
DIFFICULT SLEEPING	① ② ③ ④ ⑤ ⑥ ⑦ ⑧ ⑨ ⑩

IMPULSIVITY

ACTING WITHOUT THINKING	① ② ③ ④ ⑤ ⑥ ⑦ ⑧ ⑨ ⑩
INTERRUPTING OTHERS	① ② ③ ④ ⑤ ⑥ ⑦ ⑧ ⑨ ⑩
EASILY FRUSTRATED	① ② ③ ④ ⑤ ⑥ ⑦ ⑧ ⑨ ⑩
UNABLE TO HOLD BACK EMOTIONS	① ② ③ ④ ⑤ ⑥ ⑦ ⑧ ⑨ ⑩

MEALS

MEDICATIONS

Water Tracker

NOTES

<table>
<tr><td>

DAY GOALS

1 ....
2 ....
3 ....

</td><td>

DATE

WEEK

LOCATION

WEIGHT

</td></tr>
</table>

Mood Tracker

BEHAVIOR

INATTENTION

SHORT ATTENTION	① ② ③ ④ ⑤ ⑥ ⑦ ⑧ ⑨ ⑩
UNMOTIVATED / BORED	① ② ③ ④ ⑤ ⑥ ⑦ ⑧ ⑨ ⑩
SHORT ATTENTION	① ② ③ ④ ⑤ ⑥ ⑦ ⑧ ⑨ ⑩
FORGETFUL / CONFUSIONED	① ② ③ ④ ⑤ ⑥ ⑦ ⑧ ⑨ ⑩

HYPERACTIVITY

CONSTANTLY MOVING / TALKING	① ② ③ ④ ⑤ ⑥ ⑦ ⑧ ⑨ ⑩
STRUGGLING TO SIT STILL	① ② ③ ④ ⑤ ⑥ ⑦ ⑧ ⑨ ⑩
TOUCHING THINGS REPEATEDLY	① ② ③ ④ ⑤ ⑥ ⑦ ⑧ ⑨ ⑩
DIFFICULT SLEEPING	① ② ③ ④ ⑤ ⑥ ⑦ ⑧ ⑨ ⑩

IMPULSIVITY

ACTING WITHOUT THINKING	① ② ③ ④ ⑤ ⑥ ⑦ ⑧ ⑨ ⑩
INTERRUPTING OTHERS	① ② ③ ④ ⑤ ⑥ ⑦ ⑧ ⑨ ⑩
EASILY FRUSTRATED	① ② ③ ④ ⑤ ⑥ ⑦ ⑧ ⑨ ⑩
UNABLE TO HOLD BACK EMOTIONS	① ② ③ ④ ⑤ ⑥ ⑦ ⑧ ⑨ ⑩

MEALS

MEDICATIONS

Water Tracker

NOTES

....
....

<table>
<tr><td>

DAY GOALS

1 ....
2 ....
3 ....

</td><td>

DATE

WEEK

LOCATION

WEIGHT

</td></tr>
</table>

Mood Tracker

BEHAVIOR

INATTENTION

SHORT ATTENTION	① ② ③ ④ ⑤ ⑥ ⑦ ⑧ ⑨ ⑩
UNMOTIVATED / BORED	① ② ③ ④ ⑤ ⑥ ⑦ ⑧ ⑨ ⑩
SHORT ATTENTION	① ② ③ ④ ⑤ ⑥ ⑦ ⑧ ⑨ ⑩
FORGETFUL / CONFUSIONED	① ② ③ ④ ⑤ ⑥ ⑦ ⑧ ⑨ ⑩

HYPERACTIVITY

CONSTANTLY MOVING / TALKING	① ② ③ ④ ⑤ ⑥ ⑦ ⑧ ⑨ ⑩
STRUGGLING TO SIT STILL	① ② ③ ④ ⑤ ⑥ ⑦ ⑧ ⑨ ⑩
TOUCHING THINGS REPEATEDLY	① ② ③ ④ ⑤ ⑥ ⑦ ⑧ ⑨ ⑩
DIFFICULT SLEEPING	① ② ③ ④ ⑤ ⑥ ⑦ ⑧ ⑨ ⑩

IMPULSIVITY

ACTING WITHOUT THINKING	① ② ③ ④ ⑤ ⑥ ⑦ ⑧ ⑨ ⑩
INTERRUPTING OTHERS	① ② ③ ④ ⑤ ⑥ ⑦ ⑧ ⑨ ⑩
EASILY FRUSTRATED	① ② ③ ④ ⑤ ⑥ ⑦ ⑧ ⑨ ⑩
UNABLE TO HOLD BACK EMOTIONS	① ② ③ ④ ⑤ ⑥ ⑦ ⑧ ⑨ ⑩

MEALS

MEDICATIONS

Water Tracker

NOTES

....

....

<table>
<tr><td>

DAY GOALS

1 ....
2 ....
3 ....

</td><td>

DATE

WEEK

LOCATION

WEIGHT

</td></tr>
</table>

Mood Tracker

BEHAVIOR

INATTENTION

SHORT ATTENTION	① ② ③ ④ ⑤ ⑥ ⑦ ⑧ ⑨ ⑩
UNMOTIVATED / BORED	① ② ③ ④ ⑤ ⑥ ⑦ ⑧ ⑨ ⑩
SHORT ATTENTION	① ② ③ ④ ⑤ ⑥ ⑦ ⑧ ⑨ ⑩
FORGETFUL / CONFUSIONED	① ② ③ ④ ⑤ ⑥ ⑦ ⑧ ⑨ ⑩

HYPERACTIVITY

CONSTANTLY MOVING / TALKING	① ② ③ ④ ⑤ ⑥ ⑦ ⑧ ⑨ ⑩
STRUGGLING TO SIT STILL	① ② ③ ④ ⑤ ⑥ ⑦ ⑧ ⑨ ⑩
TOUCHING THINGS REPEATEDLY	① ② ③ ④ ⑤ ⑥ ⑦ ⑧ ⑨ ⑩
DIFFICULT SLEEPING	① ② ③ ④ ⑤ ⑥ ⑦ ⑧ ⑨ ⑩

IMPULSIVITY

ACTING WITHOUT THINKING	① ② ③ ④ ⑤ ⑥ ⑦ ⑧ ⑨ ⑩
INTERRUPTING OTHERS	① ② ③ ④ ⑤ ⑥ ⑦ ⑧ ⑨ ⑩
EASILY FRUSTRATED	① ② ③ ④ ⑤ ⑥ ⑦ ⑧ ⑨ ⑩
UNABLE TO HOLD BACK EMOTIONS	① ② ③ ④ ⑤ ⑥ ⑦ ⑧ ⑨ ⑩

MEALS

MEDICATIONS

Water Tracker

NOTES

....
....

Mood Tracker

BEHAVIOR

INATTENTION

SHORT ATTENTION	① ② ③ ④ ⑤ ⑥ ⑦ ⑧ ⑨ ⑩
UNMOTIVATED / BORED	① ② ③ ④ ⑤ ⑥ ⑦ ⑧ ⑨ ⑩
SHORT ATTENTION	① ② ③ ④ ⑤ ⑥ ⑦ ⑧ ⑨ ⑩
FORGETFUL / CONFUSIONED	① ② ③ ④ ⑤ ⑥ ⑦ ⑧ ⑨ ⑩

HYPERACTIVITY

CONSTANTLY MOVING / TALKING	① ② ③ ④ ⑤ ⑥ ⑦ ⑧ ⑨ ⑩
STRUGGLING TO SIT STILL	① ② ③ ④ ⑤ ⑥ ⑦ ⑧ ⑨ ⑩
TOUCHING THINGS REPEATEDLY	① ② ③ ④ ⑤ ⑥ ⑦ ⑧ ⑨ ⑩
DIFFICULT SLEEPING	① ② ③ ④ ⑤ ⑥ ⑦ ⑧ ⑨ ⑩

IMPULSIVITY

ACTING WITHOUT THINKING	① ② ③ ④ ⑤ ⑥ ⑦ ⑧ ⑨ ⑩
INTERRUPTING OTHERS	① ② ③ ④ ⑤ ⑥ ⑦ ⑧ ⑨ ⑩
EASILY FRUSTRATED	① ② ③ ④ ⑤ ⑥ ⑦ ⑧ ⑨ ⑩
UNABLE TO HOLD BACK EMOTIONS	① ② ③ ④ ⑤ ⑥ ⑦ ⑧ ⑨ ⑩

MEALS

MEDICATIONS

Water Tracker

NOTES

<table>
<tr><td>

DAY GOALS

1 ....
2 ....
3 ....

</td><td>

DATE

WEEK

LOCATION

WEIGHT

</td></tr>
</table>

Mood Tracker

BEHAVIOR

INATTENTION

SHORT ATTENTION	① ② ③ ④ ⑤ ⑥ ⑦ ⑧ ⑨ ⑩
UNMOTIVATED / BORED	① ② ③ ④ ⑤ ⑥ ⑦ ⑧ ⑨ ⑩
SHORT ATTENTION	① ② ③ ④ ⑤ ⑥ ⑦ ⑧ ⑨ ⑩
FORGETFUL / CONFUSIONED	① ② ③ ④ ⑤ ⑥ ⑦ ⑧ ⑨ ⑩

HYPERACTIVITY

CONSTANTLY MOVING / TALKING	① ② ③ ④ ⑤ ⑥ ⑦ ⑧ ⑨ ⑩
STRUGGLING TO SIT STILL	① ② ③ ④ ⑤ ⑥ ⑦ ⑧ ⑨ ⑩
TOUCHING THINGS REPEATEDLY	① ② ③ ④ ⑤ ⑥ ⑦ ⑧ ⑨ ⑩
DIFFICULT SLEEPING	① ② ③ ④ ⑤ ⑥ ⑦ ⑧ ⑨ ⑩

IMPULSIVITY

ACTING WITHOUT THINKING	① ② ③ ④ ⑤ ⑥ ⑦ ⑧ ⑨ ⑩
INTERRUPTING OTHERS	① ② ③ ④ ⑤ ⑥ ⑦ ⑧ ⑨ ⑩
EASILY FRUSTRATED	① ② ③ ④ ⑤ ⑥ ⑦ ⑧ ⑨ ⑩
UNABLE TO HOLD BACK EMOTIONS	① ② ③ ④ ⑤ ⑥ ⑦ ⑧ ⑨ ⑩

MEALS

MEDICATIONS

Water Tracker

NOTES

....

....

<table>
<tr><td>

DAY GOALS

1 ....
2 ....
3 ....

</td><td>

DATE

WEEK

LOCATION

WEIGHT

</td></tr>
</table>

Mood Tracker

BEHAVIOR

INATTENTION

SHORT ATTENTION	① ② ③ ④ ⑤ ⑥ ⑦ ⑧ ⑨ ⑩
UNMOTIVATED / BORED	① ② ③ ④ ⑤ ⑥ ⑦ ⑧ ⑨ ⑩
SHORT ATTENTION	① ② ③ ④ ⑤ ⑥ ⑦ ⑧ ⑨ ⑩
FORGETFUL / CONFUSIONED	① ② ③ ④ ⑤ ⑥ ⑦ ⑧ ⑨ ⑩

HYPERACTIVITY

CONSTANTLY MOVING / TALKING	① ② ③ ④ ⑤ ⑥ ⑦ ⑧ ⑨ ⑩
STRUGGLING TO SIT STILL	① ② ③ ④ ⑤ ⑥ ⑦ ⑧ ⑨ ⑩
TOUCHING THINGS REPEATEDLY	① ② ③ ④ ⑤ ⑥ ⑦ ⑧ ⑨ ⑩
DIFFICULT SLEEPING	① ② ③ ④ ⑤ ⑥ ⑦ ⑧ ⑨ ⑩

IMPULSIVITY

ACTING WITHOUT THINKING	① ② ③ ④ ⑤ ⑥ ⑦ ⑧ ⑨ ⑩
INTERRUPTING OTHERS	① ② ③ ④ ⑤ ⑥ ⑦ ⑧ ⑨ ⑩
EASILY FRUSTRATED	① ② ③ ④ ⑤ ⑥ ⑦ ⑧ ⑨ ⑩
UNABLE TO HOLD BACK EMOTIONS	① ② ③ ④ ⑤ ⑥ ⑦ ⑧ ⑨ ⑩

MEALS	MEDICATIONS

Water Tracker

NOTES

....
....

<table>
<tr><td>

DAY GOALS

1 ....
2 ....
3 ....

</td><td>

DATE
WEEK
LOCATION
WEIGHT

</td></tr>
</table>

Mood Tracker ☹ 😐 😖 😢 😠 😃

BEHAVIOR

INATTENTION

SHORT ATTENTION	① ② ③ ④ ⑤ ⑥ ⑦ ⑧ ⑨ ⑩
UNMOTIVATED / BORED	① ② ③ ④ ⑤ ⑥ ⑦ ⑧ ⑨ ⑩
SHORT ATTENTION	① ② ③ ④ ⑤ ⑥ ⑦ ⑧ ⑨ ⑩
FORGETFUL / CONFUSIONED	① ② ③ ④ ⑤ ⑥ ⑦ ⑧ ⑨ ⑩

HYPERACTIVITY

CONSTANTLY MOVING / TALKING	① ② ③ ④ ⑤ ⑥ ⑦ ⑧ ⑨ ⑩
STRUGGLING TO SIT STILL	① ② ③ ④ ⑤ ⑥ ⑦ ⑧ ⑨ ⑩
TOUCHING THINGS REPEATEDLY	① ② ③ ④ ⑤ ⑥ ⑦ ⑧ ⑨ ⑩
DIFFICULT SLEEPING	① ② ③ ④ ⑤ ⑥ ⑦ ⑧ ⑨ ⑩

IMPULSIVITY

ACTING WITHOUT THINKING	① ② ③ ④ ⑤ ⑥ ⑦ ⑧ ⑨ ⑩
INTERRUPTING OTHERS	① ② ③ ④ ⑤ ⑥ ⑦ ⑧ ⑨ ⑩
EASILY FRUSTRATED	① ② ③ ④ ⑤ ⑥ ⑦ ⑧ ⑨ ⑩
UNABLE TO HOLD BACK EMOTIONS	① ② ③ ④ ⑤ ⑥ ⑦ ⑧ ⑨ ⑩

MEALS	MEDICATIONS

Water Tracker 🍼 🍼 🍼 🍼 🍼 🍼 🍼 🍼

NOTES

....
....

<table>
<tr><td>

DAY GOALS

1 ....
2 ....
3 ....

</td><td>

DATE

WEEK

LOCATION

WEIGHT

</td></tr>
</table>

Mood Tracker

BEHAVIOR

INATTENTION

SHORT ATTENTION	① ② ③ ④ ⑤ ⑥ ⑦ ⑧ ⑨ ⑩
UNMOTIVATED / BORED	① ② ③ ④ ⑤ ⑥ ⑦ ⑧ ⑨ ⑩
SHORT ATTENTION	① ② ③ ④ ⑤ ⑥ ⑦ ⑧ ⑨ ⑩
FORGETFUL / CONFUSIONED	① ② ③ ④ ⑤ ⑥ ⑦ ⑧ ⑨ ⑩

HYPERACTIVITY

CONSTANTLY MOVING / TALKING	① ② ③ ④ ⑤ ⑥ ⑦ ⑧ ⑨ ⑩
STRUGGLING TO SIT STILL	① ② ③ ④ ⑤ ⑥ ⑦ ⑧ ⑨ ⑩
TOUCHING THINGS REPEATEDLY	① ② ③ ④ ⑤ ⑥ ⑦ ⑧ ⑨ ⑩
DIFFICULT SLEEPING	① ② ③ ④ ⑤ ⑥ ⑦ ⑧ ⑨ ⑩

IMPULSIVITY

ACTING WITHOUT THINKING	① ② ③ ④ ⑤ ⑥ ⑦ ⑧ ⑨ ⑩
INTERRUPTING OTHERS	① ② ③ ④ ⑤ ⑥ ⑦ ⑧ ⑨ ⑩
EASILY FRUSTRATED	① ② ③ ④ ⑤ ⑥ ⑦ ⑧ ⑨ ⑩
UNABLE TO HOLD BACK EMOTIONS	① ② ③ ④ ⑤ ⑥ ⑦ ⑧ ⑨ ⑩

MEALS	MEDICATIONS

Water Tracker

NOTES

....
....

DATE

WEEK

LOCATION

WEIGHT

Mood Tracker

BEHAVIOR

INATTENTION

SHORT ATTENTION	1 2 3 4 5 6 7 8 9 10
UNMOTIVATED / BORED	1 2 3 4 5 6 7 8 9 10
SHORT ATTENTION	1 2 3 4 5 6 7 8 9 10
FORGETFUL / CONFUSIONED	1 2 3 4 5 6 7 8 9 10

HYPERACTIVITY

CONSTANTLY MOVING / TALKING	1 2 3 4 5 6 7 8 9 10
STRUGGLING TO SIT STILL	1 2 3 4 5 6 7 8 9 10
TOUCHING THINGS REPEATEDLY	1 2 3 4 5 6 7 8 9 10
DIFFICULT SLEEPING	1 2 3 4 5 6 7 8 9 10

IMPULSIVITY

ACTING WITHOUT THINKING	1 2 3 4 5 6 7 8 9 10
INTERRUPTING OTHERS	1 2 3 4 5 6 7 8 9 10
EASILY FRUSTRATED	1 2 3 4 5 6 7 8 9 10
UNABLE TO HOLD BACK EMOTIONS	1 2 3 4 5 6 7 8 9 10

MEALS

MEDICATIONS

Water Tracker

NOTES

<table>
<tr><td>

DAY GOALS

1 ....

2 ....

3 ....

</td><td>

DATE

WEEK

LOCATION

WEIGHT

</td></tr>
</table>

Mood Tracker

BEHAVIOR

INATTENTION

SHORT ATTENTION	① ② ③ ④ ⑤ ⑥ ⑦ ⑧ ⑨ ⑩
UNMOTIVATED / BORED	① ② ③ ④ ⑤ ⑥ ⑦ ⑧ ⑨ ⑩
SHORT ATTENTION	① ② ③ ④ ⑤ ⑥ ⑦ ⑧ ⑨ ⑩
FORGETFUL / CONFUSIONED	① ② ③ ④ ⑤ ⑥ ⑦ ⑧ ⑨ ⑩

HYPERACTIVITY

CONSTANTLY MOVING / TALKING	① ② ③ ④ ⑤ ⑥ ⑦ ⑧ ⑨ ⑩
STRUGGLING TO SIT STILL	① ② ③ ④ ⑤ ⑥ ⑦ ⑧ ⑨ ⑩
TOUCHING THINGS REPEATEDLY	① ② ③ ④ ⑤ ⑥ ⑦ ⑧ ⑨ ⑩
DIFFICULT SLEEPING	① ② ③ ④ ⑤ ⑥ ⑦ ⑧ ⑨ ⑩

IMPULSIVITY

ACTING WITHOUT THINKING	① ② ③ ④ ⑤ ⑥ ⑦ ⑧ ⑨ ⑩
INTERRUPTING OTHERS	① ② ③ ④ ⑤ ⑥ ⑦ ⑧ ⑨ ⑩
EASILY FRUSTRATED	① ② ③ ④ ⑤ ⑥ ⑦ ⑧ ⑨ ⑩
UNABLE TO HOLD BACK EMOTIONS	① ② ③ ④ ⑤ ⑥ ⑦ ⑧ ⑨ ⑩

MEALS	MEDICATIONS

Water Tracker

NOTES

....

....

<table>
<tr><td>

DAY GOALS

1 ....
2 ....
3 ....

</td><td>

DATE

WEEK

LOCATION

WEIGHT

</td></tr>
</table>

Mood Tracker

BEHAVIOR

INATTENTION

SHORT ATTENTION	① ② ③ ④ ⑤ ⑥ ⑦ ⑧ ⑨ ⑩
UNMOTIVATED / BORED	① ② ③ ④ ⑤ ⑥ ⑦ ⑧ ⑨ ⑩
SHORT ATTENTION	① ② ③ ④ ⑤ ⑥ ⑦ ⑧ ⑨ ⑩
FORGETFUL / CONFUSIONED	① ② ③ ④ ⑤ ⑥ ⑦ ⑧ ⑨ ⑩

HYPERACTIVITY

CONSTANTLY MOVING / TALKING	① ② ③ ④ ⑤ ⑥ ⑦ ⑧ ⑨ ⑩
STRUGGLING TO SIT STILL	① ② ③ ④ ⑤ ⑥ ⑦ ⑧ ⑨ ⑩
TOUCHING THINGS REPEATEDLY	① ② ③ ④ ⑤ ⑥ ⑦ ⑧ ⑨ ⑩
DIFFICULT SLEEPING	① ② ③ ④ ⑤ ⑥ ⑦ ⑧ ⑨ ⑩

IMPULSIVITY

ACTING WITHOUT THINKING	① ② ③ ④ ⑤ ⑥ ⑦ ⑧ ⑨ ⑩
INTERRUPTING OTHERS	① ② ③ ④ ⑤ ⑥ ⑦ ⑧ ⑨ ⑩
EASILY FRUSTRATED	① ② ③ ④ ⑤ ⑥ ⑦ ⑧ ⑨ ⑩
UNABLE TO HOLD BACK EMOTIONS	① ② ③ ④ ⑤ ⑥ ⑦ ⑧ ⑨ ⑩

MEALS

MEDICATIONS

Water Tracker

NOTES

....
....

DAY GOALS

1 ....
2 ....
3 ....

DATE

WEEK

LOCATION

WEIGHT

Mood Tracker

BEHAVIOR

INATTENTION

SHORT ATTENTION	① ② ③ ④ ⑤ ⑥ ⑦ ⑧ ⑨ ⑩
UNMOTIVATED / BORED	① ② ③ ④ ⑤ ⑥ ⑦ ⑧ ⑨ ⑩
SHORT ATTENTION	① ② ③ ④ ⑤ ⑥ ⑦ ⑧ ⑨ ⑩
FORGETFUL / CONFUSIONED	① ② ③ ④ ⑤ ⑥ ⑦ ⑧ ⑨ ⑩

HYPERACTIVITY

CONSTANTLY MOVING / TALKING	① ② ③ ④ ⑤ ⑥ ⑦ ⑧ ⑨ ⑩
STRUGGLING TO SIT STILL	① ② ③ ④ ⑤ ⑥ ⑦ ⑧ ⑨ ⑩
TOUCHING THINGS REPEATEDLY	① ② ③ ④ ⑤ ⑥ ⑦ ⑧ ⑨ ⑩
DIFFICULT SLEEPING	① ② ③ ④ ⑤ ⑥ ⑦ ⑧ ⑨ ⑩

IMPULSIVITY

ACTING WITHOUT THINKING	① ② ③ ④ ⑤ ⑥ ⑦ ⑧ ⑨ ⑩
INTERRUPTING OTHERS	① ② ③ ④ ⑤ ⑥ ⑦ ⑧ ⑨ ⑩
EASILY FRUSTRATED	① ② ③ ④ ⑤ ⑥ ⑦ ⑧ ⑨ ⑩
UNABLE TO HOLD BACK EMOTIONS	① ② ③ ④ ⑤ ⑥ ⑦ ⑧ ⑨ ⑩

MEALS

MEDICATIONS

Water Tracker

NOTES

....
....

<table>
<tr><td>

DAY GOALS

1 ....
2 ....
3 ....

</td><td>

DATE

WEEK

LOCATION

WEIGHT

</td></tr>
</table>

Mood Tracker

BEHAVIOR

INATTENTION

SHORT ATTENTION	① ② ③ ④ ⑤ ⑥ ⑦ ⑧ ⑨ ⑩
UNMOTIVATED / BORED	① ② ③ ④ ⑤ ⑥ ⑦ ⑧ ⑨ ⑩
SHORT ATTENTION	① ② ③ ④ ⑤ ⑥ ⑦ ⑧ ⑨ ⑩
FORGETFUL / CONFUSIONED	① ② ③ ④ ⑤ ⑥ ⑦ ⑧ ⑨ ⑩

HYPERACTIVITY

CONSTANTLY MOVING / TALKING	① ② ③ ④ ⑤ ⑥ ⑦ ⑧ ⑨ ⑩
STRUGGLING TO SIT STILL	① ② ③ ④ ⑤ ⑥ ⑦ ⑧ ⑨ ⑩
TOUCHING THINGS REPEATEDLY	① ② ③ ④ ⑤ ⑥ ⑦ ⑧ ⑨ ⑩
DIFFICULT SLEEPING	① ② ③ ④ ⑤ ⑥ ⑦ ⑧ ⑨ ⑩

IMPULSIVITY

ACTING WITHOUT THINKING	① ② ③ ④ ⑤ ⑥ ⑦ ⑧ ⑨ ⑩
INTERRUPTING OTHERS	① ② ③ ④ ⑤ ⑥ ⑦ ⑧ ⑨ ⑩
EASILY FRUSTRATED	① ② ③ ④ ⑤ ⑥ ⑦ ⑧ ⑨ ⑩
UNABLE TO HOLD BACK EMOTIONS	① ② ③ ④ ⑤ ⑥ ⑦ ⑧ ⑨ ⑩

MEALS	MEDICATIONS

Water Tracker

NOTES

....
....

<table>
<tr><td>

DAY GOALS

1 ....
2 ....
3 ....

</td><td>

DATE

WEEK

LOCATION

WEIGHT

</td></tr>
</table>

Mood Tracker

BEHAVIOR

INATTENTION

SHORT ATTENTION	① ② ③ ④ ⑤ ⑥ ⑦ ⑧ ⑨ ⑩
UNMOTIVATED / BORED	① ② ③ ④ ⑤ ⑥ ⑦ ⑧ ⑨ ⑩
SHORT ATTENTION	① ② ③ ④ ⑤ ⑥ ⑦ ⑧ ⑨ ⑩
FORGETFUL / CONFUSIONED	① ② ③ ④ ⑤ ⑥ ⑦ ⑧ ⑨ ⑩

HYPERACTIVITY

CONSTANTLY MOVING / TALKING	① ② ③ ④ ⑤ ⑥ ⑦ ⑧ ⑨ ⑩
STRUGGLING TO SIT STILL	① ② ③ ④ ⑤ ⑥ ⑦ ⑧ ⑨ ⑩
TOUCHING THINGS REPEATEDLY	① ② ③ ④ ⑤ ⑥ ⑦ ⑧ ⑨ ⑩
DIFFICULT SLEEPING	① ② ③ ④ ⑤ ⑥ ⑦ ⑧ ⑨ ⑩

IMPULSIVITY

ACTING WITHOUT THINKING	① ② ③ ④ ⑤ ⑥ ⑦ ⑧ ⑨ ⑩
INTERRUPTING OTHERS	① ② ③ ④ ⑤ ⑥ ⑦ ⑧ ⑨ ⑩
EASILY FRUSTRATED	① ② ③ ④ ⑤ ⑥ ⑦ ⑧ ⑨ ⑩
UNABLE TO HOLD BACK EMOTIONS	① ② ③ ④ ⑤ ⑥ ⑦ ⑧ ⑨ ⑩

MEALS

MEDICATIONS

Water Tracker

NOTES

....
....

1 ....
2 ....
3 ....

DATE

WEEK

LOCATION

WEIGHT

Mood Tracker

BEHAVIOR

INATTENTION

SHORT ATTENTION	① ② ③ ④ ⑤ ⑥ ⑦ ⑧ ⑨ ⑩
UNMOTIVATED / BORED	① ② ③ ④ ⑤ ⑥ ⑦ ⑧ ⑨ ⑩
SHORT ATTENTION	① ② ③ ④ ⑤ ⑥ ⑦ ⑧ ⑨ ⑩
FORGETFUL / CONFUSIONED	① ② ③ ④ ⑤ ⑥ ⑦ ⑧ ⑨ ⑩

HYPERACTIVITY

CONSTANTLY MOVING / TALKING	① ② ③ ④ ⑤ ⑥ ⑦ ⑧ ⑨ ⑩
STRUGGLING TO SIT STILL	① ② ③ ④ ⑤ ⑥ ⑦ ⑧ ⑨ ⑩
TOUCHING THINGS REPEATEDLY	① ② ③ ④ ⑤ ⑥ ⑦ ⑧ ⑨ ⑩
DIFFICULT SLEEPING	① ② ③ ④ ⑤ ⑥ ⑦ ⑧ ⑨ ⑩

IMPULSIVITY

ACTING WITHOUT THINKING	① ② ③ ④ ⑤ ⑥ ⑦ ⑧ ⑨ ⑩
INTERRUPTING OTHERS	① ② ③ ④ ⑤ ⑥ ⑦ ⑧ ⑨ ⑩
EASILY FRUSTRATED	① ② ③ ④ ⑤ ⑥ ⑦ ⑧ ⑨ ⑩
UNABLE TO HOLD BACK EMOTIONS	① ② ③ ④ ⑤ ⑥ ⑦ ⑧ ⑨ ⑩

MEALS

MEDICATIONS

Water Tracker

NOTES

....
....

DAY GOALS

1 ....
2 ....
3 ....

DATE

WEEK

LOCATION

WEIGHT

Mood Tracker

BEHAVIOR

INATTENTION

SHORT ATTENTION	1 2 3 4 5 6 7 8 9 10
UNMOTIVATED / BORED	1 2 3 4 5 6 7 8 9 10
SHORT ATTENTION	1 2 3 4 5 6 7 8 9 10
FORGETFUL / CONFUSIONED	1 2 3 4 5 6 7 8 9 10

HYPERACTIVITY

CONSTANTLY MOVING / TALKING	1 2 3 4 5 6 7 8 9 10
STRUGGLING TO SIT STILL	1 2 3 4 5 6 7 8 9 10
TOUCHING THINGS REPEATEDLY	1 2 3 4 5 6 7 8 9 10
DIFFICULT SLEEPING	1 2 3 4 5 6 7 8 9 10

IMPULSIVITY

ACTING WITHOUT THINKING	1 2 3 4 5 6 7 8 9 10
INTERRUPTING OTHERS	1 2 3 4 5 6 7 8 9 10
EASILY FRUSTRATED	1 2 3 4 5 6 7 8 9 10
UNABLE TO HOLD BACK EMOTIONS	1 2 3 4 5 6 7 8 9 10

MEALS

MEDICATIONS

Water Tracker

NOTES

....
....

DAY GOALS

1 ....
2 ....
3 ....

DATE

WEEK

LOCATION

WEIGHT

Mood Tracker

BEHAVIOR

INATTENTION

SHORT ATTENTION	① ② ③ ④ ⑤ ⑥ ⑦ ⑧ ⑨ ⑩
UNMOTIVATED / BORED	① ② ③ ④ ⑤ ⑥ ⑦ ⑧ ⑨ ⑩
SHORT ATTENTION	① ② ③ ④ ⑤ ⑥ ⑦ ⑧ ⑨ ⑩
FORGETFUL / CONFUSIONED	① ② ③ ④ ⑤ ⑥ ⑦ ⑧ ⑨ ⑩

HYPERACTIVITY

CONSTANTLY MOVING / TALKING	① ② ③ ④ ⑤ ⑥ ⑦ ⑧ ⑨ ⑩
STRUGGLING TO SIT STILL	① ② ③ ④ ⑤ ⑥ ⑦ ⑧ ⑨ ⑩
TOUCHING THINGS REPEATEDLY	① ② ③ ④ ⑤ ⑥ ⑦ ⑧ ⑨ ⑩
DIFFICULT SLEEPING	① ② ③ ④ ⑤ ⑥ ⑦ ⑧ ⑨ ⑩

IMPULSIVITY

ACTING WITHOUT THINKING	① ② ③ ④ ⑤ ⑥ ⑦ ⑧ ⑨ ⑩
INTERRUPTING OTHERS	① ② ③ ④ ⑤ ⑥ ⑦ ⑧ ⑨ ⑩
EASILY FRUSTRATED	① ② ③ ④ ⑤ ⑥ ⑦ ⑧ ⑨ ⑩
UNABLE TO HOLD BACK EMOTIONS	① ② ③ ④ ⑤ ⑥ ⑦ ⑧ ⑨ ⑩

MEALS

MEDICATIONS

Water Tracker

NOTES

....
....

<table>
<tr><td>

DAY GOALS

1 ....
2 ....
3 ....

</td><td>

DATE

WEEK

LOCATION

WEIGHT

</td></tr>
</table>

Mood Tracker 😦 😐 😣 😢 😠 😃

BEHAVIOR

INATTENTION

SHORT ATTENTION	① ② ③ ④ ⑤ ⑥ ⑦ ⑧ ⑨ ⑩
UNMOTIVATED / BORED	① ② ③ ④ ⑤ ⑥ ⑦ ⑧ ⑨ ⑩
SHORT ATTENTION	① ② ③ ④ ⑤ ⑥ ⑦ ⑧ ⑨ ⑩
FORGETFUL / CONFUSIONED	① ② ③ ④ ⑤ ⑥ ⑦ ⑧ ⑨ ⑩

HYPERACTIVITY

CONSTANTLY MOVING / TALKING	① ② ③ ④ ⑤ ⑥ ⑦ ⑧ ⑨ ⑩
STRUGGLING TO SIT STILL	① ② ③ ④ ⑤ ⑥ ⑦ ⑧ ⑨ ⑩
TOUCHING THINGS REPEATEDLY	① ② ③ ④ ⑤ ⑥ ⑦ ⑧ ⑨ ⑩
DIFFICULT SLEEPING	① ② ③ ④ ⑤ ⑥ ⑦ ⑧ ⑨ ⑩

IMPULSIVITY

ACTING WITHOUT THINKING	① ② ③ ④ ⑤ ⑥ ⑦ ⑧ ⑨ ⑩
INTERRUPTING OTHERS	① ② ③ ④ ⑤ ⑥ ⑦ ⑧ ⑨ ⑩
EASILY FRUSTRATED	① ② ③ ④ ⑤ ⑥ ⑦ ⑧ ⑨ ⑩
UNABLE TO HOLD BACK EMOTIONS	① ② ③ ④ ⑤ ⑥ ⑦ ⑧ ⑨ ⑩

MEALS	MEDICATIONS

Water Tracker 🍶 🍶 🍶 🍶 🍶 🍶 🍶 🍶

NOTES

....
....

DAY GOALS

1 ....
2 ....
3 ....

DATE

WEEK

LOCATION

WEIGHT

Mood Tracker

BEHAVIOR

INATTENTION

SHORT ATTENTION	① ② ③ ④ ⑤ ⑥ ⑦ ⑧ ⑨ ⑩
UNMOTIVATED / BORED	① ② ③ ④ ⑤ ⑥ ⑦ ⑧ ⑨ ⑩
SHORT ATTENTION	① ② ③ ④ ⑤ ⑥ ⑦ ⑧ ⑨ ⑩
FORGETFUL / CONFUSIONED	① ② ③ ④ ⑤ ⑥ ⑦ ⑧ ⑨ ⑩

HYPERACTIVITY

CONSTANTLY MOVING / TALKING	① ② ③ ④ ⑤ ⑥ ⑦ ⑧ ⑨ ⑩
STRUGGLING TO SIT STILL	① ② ③ ④ ⑤ ⑥ ⑦ ⑧ ⑨ ⑩
TOUCHING THINGS REPEATEDLY	① ② ③ ④ ⑤ ⑥ ⑦ ⑧ ⑨ ⑩
DIFFICULT SLEEPING	① ② ③ ④ ⑤ ⑥ ⑦ ⑧ ⑨ ⑩

IMPULSIVITY

ACTING WITHOUT THINKING	① ② ③ ④ ⑤ ⑥ ⑦ ⑧ ⑨ ⑩
INTERRUPTING OTHERS	① ② ③ ④ ⑤ ⑥ ⑦ ⑧ ⑨ ⑩
EASILY FRUSTRATED	① ② ③ ④ ⑤ ⑥ ⑦ ⑧ ⑨ ⑩
UNABLE TO HOLD BACK EMOTIONS	① ② ③ ④ ⑤ ⑥ ⑦ ⑧ ⑨ ⑩

MEALS

MEDICATIONS

Water Tracker

NOTES

....
....

DATE

WEEK

LOCATION

WEIGHT

Mood Tracker

BEHAVIOR

INATTENTION

SHORT ATTENTION	1 2 3 4 5 6 7 8 9 10
UNMOTIVATED / BORED	1 2 3 4 5 6 7 8 9 10
SHORT ATTENTION	1 2 3 4 5 6 7 8 9 10
FORGETFUL / CONFUSIONED	1 2 3 4 5 6 7 8 9 10

HYPERACTIVITY

CONSTANTLY MOVING / TALKING	1 2 3 4 5 6 7 8 9 10
STRUGGLING TO SIT STILL	1 2 3 4 5 6 7 8 9 10
TOUCHING THINGS REPEATEDLY	1 2 3 4 5 6 7 8 9 10
DIFFICULT SLEEPING	1 2 3 4 5 6 7 8 9 10

IMPULSIVITY

ACTING WITHOUT THINKING	1 2 3 4 5 6 7 8 9 10
INTERRUPTING OTHERS	1 2 3 4 5 6 7 8 9 10
EASILY FRUSTRATED	1 2 3 4 5 6 7 8 9 10
UNABLE TO HOLD BACK EMOTIONS	1 2 3 4 5 6 7 8 9 10

MEALS

MEDICATIONS

Water Tracker

NOTES

Mood Tracker

BEHAVIOR

INATTENTION

SHORT ATTENTION	① ② ③ ④ ⑤ ⑥ ⑦ ⑧ ⑨ ⑩
UNMOTIVATED / BORED	① ② ③ ④ ⑤ ⑥ ⑦ ⑧ ⑨ ⑩
SHORT ATTENTION	① ② ③ ④ ⑤ ⑥ ⑦ ⑧ ⑨ ⑩
FORGETFUL / CONFUSIONED	① ② ③ ④ ⑤ ⑥ ⑦ ⑧ ⑨ ⑩

HYPERACTIVITY

CONSTANTLY MOVING / TALKING	① ② ③ ④ ⑤ ⑥ ⑦ ⑧ ⑨ ⑩
STRUGGLING TO SIT STILL	① ② ③ ④ ⑤ ⑥ ⑦ ⑧ ⑨ ⑩
TOUCHING THINGS REPEATEDLY	① ② ③ ④ ⑤ ⑥ ⑦ ⑧ ⑨ ⑩
DIFFICULT SLEEPING	① ② ③ ④ ⑤ ⑥ ⑦ ⑧ ⑨ ⑩

IMPULSIVITY

ACTING WITHOUT THINKING	① ② ③ ④ ⑤ ⑥ ⑦ ⑧ ⑨ ⑩
INTERRUPTING OTHERS	① ② ③ ④ ⑤ ⑥ ⑦ ⑧ ⑨ ⑩
EASILY FRUSTRATED	① ② ③ ④ ⑤ ⑥ ⑦ ⑧ ⑨ ⑩
UNABLE TO HOLD BACK EMOTIONS	① ② ③ ④ ⑤ ⑥ ⑦ ⑧ ⑨ ⑩

MEALS

MEDICATIONS

Water Tracker

NOTES

Mood Tracker

BEHAVIOR

INATTENTION

SHORT ATTENTION	① ② ③ ④ ⑤ ⑥ ⑦ ⑧ ⑨ ⑩
UNMOTIVATED / BORED	① ② ③ ④ ⑤ ⑥ ⑦ ⑧ ⑨ ⑩
SHORT ATTENTION	① ② ③ ④ ⑤ ⑥ ⑦ ⑧ ⑨ ⑩
FORGETFUL / CONFUSIONED	① ② ③ ④ ⑤ ⑥ ⑦ ⑧ ⑨ ⑩

HYPERACTIVITY

CONSTANTLY MOVING / TALKING	① ② ③ ④ ⑤ ⑥ ⑦ ⑧ ⑨ ⑩
STRUGGLING TO SIT STILL	① ② ③ ④ ⑤ ⑥ ⑦ ⑧ ⑨ ⑩
TOUCHING THINGS REPEATEDLY	① ② ③ ④ ⑤ ⑥ ⑦ ⑧ ⑨ ⑩
DIFFICULT SLEEPING	① ② ③ ④ ⑤ ⑥ ⑦ ⑧ ⑨ ⑩

IMPULSIVITY

ACTING WITHOUT THINKING	① ② ③ ④ ⑤ ⑥ ⑦ ⑧ ⑨ ⑩
INTERRUPTING OTHERS	① ② ③ ④ ⑤ ⑥ ⑦ ⑧ ⑨ ⑩
EASILY FRUSTRATED	① ② ③ ④ ⑤ ⑥ ⑦ ⑧ ⑨ ⑩
UNABLE TO HOLD BACK EMOTIONS	① ② ③ ④ ⑤ ⑥ ⑦ ⑧ ⑨ ⑩

MEALS

MEDICATIONS

Water Tracker

NOTES

....
....

DAY GOALS

1 ....
2 ....
3 ....

Mood Tracker

BEHAVIOR

INATTENTION

SHORT ATTENTION	① ② ③ ④ ⑤ ⑥ ⑦ ⑧ ⑨ ⑩
UNMOTIVATED / BORED	① ② ③ ④ ⑤ ⑥ ⑦ ⑧ ⑨ ⑩
SHORT ATTENTION	① ② ③ ④ ⑤ ⑥ ⑦ ⑧ ⑨ ⑩
FORGETFUL / CONFUSIONED	① ② ③ ④ ⑤ ⑥ ⑦ ⑧ ⑨ ⑩

HYPERACTIVITY

CONSTANTLY MOVING / TALKING	① ② ③ ④ ⑤ ⑥ ⑦ ⑧ ⑨ ⑩
STRUGGLING TO SIT STILL	① ② ③ ④ ⑤ ⑥ ⑦ ⑧ ⑨ ⑩
TOUCHING THINGS REPEATEDLY	① ② ③ ④ ⑤ ⑥ ⑦ ⑧ ⑨ ⑩
DIFFICULT SLEEPING	① ② ③ ④ ⑤ ⑥ ⑦ ⑧ ⑨ ⑩

IMPULSIVITY

ACTING WITHOUT THINKING	① ② ③ ④ ⑤ ⑥ ⑦ ⑧ ⑨ ⑩
INTERRUPTING OTHERS	① ② ③ ④ ⑤ ⑥ ⑦ ⑧ ⑨ ⑩
EASILY FRUSTRATED	① ② ③ ④ ⑤ ⑥ ⑦ ⑧ ⑨ ⑩
UNABLE TO HOLD BACK EMOTIONS	① ② ③ ④ ⑤ ⑥ ⑦ ⑧ ⑨ ⑩

MEALS

MEDICATIONS

Water Tracker

NOTES

....
....

Mood Tracker

BEHAVIOR

INATTENTION

SHORT ATTENTION	1 2 3 4 5 6 7 8 9 10
UNMOTIVATED / BORED	1 2 3 4 5 6 7 8 9 10
SHORT ATTENTION	1 2 3 4 5 6 7 8 9 10
FORGETFUL / CONFUSIONED	1 2 3 4 5 6 7 8 9 10

HYPERACTIVITY

CONSTANTLY MOVING / TALKING	1 2 3 4 5 6 7 8 9 10
STRUGGLING TO SIT STILL	1 2 3 4 5 6 7 8 9 10
TOUCHING THINGS REPEATEDLY	1 2 3 4 5 6 7 8 9 10
DIFFICULT SLEEPING	1 2 3 4 5 6 7 8 9 10

IMPULSIVITY

ACTING WITHOUT THINKING	1 2 3 4 5 6 7 8 9 10
INTERRUPTING OTHERS	1 2 3 4 5 6 7 8 9 10
EASILY FRUSTRATED	1 2 3 4 5 6 7 8 9 10
UNABLE TO HOLD BACK EMOTIONS	1 2 3 4 5 6 7 8 9 10

MEALS

MEDICATIONS

Water Tracker

NOTES

<table>
<tr><td>

DAY GOALS

1 ....
2 ....
3 ....

</td><td>

DATE

WEEK

LOCATION

WEIGHT

</td></tr>
</table>

Mood Tracker 😟 😐 😖 😢 😠 😃

BEHAVIOR

INATTENTION

SHORT ATTENTION	① ② ③ ④ ⑤ ⑥ ⑦ ⑧ ⑨ ⑩
UNMOTIVATED / BORED	① ② ③ ④ ⑤ ⑥ ⑦ ⑧ ⑨ ⑩
SHORT ATTENTION	① ② ③ ④ ⑤ ⑥ ⑦ ⑧ ⑨ ⑩
FORGETFUL / CONFUSIONED	① ② ③ ④ ⑤ ⑥ ⑦ ⑧ ⑨ ⑩

HYPERACTIVITY

CONSTANTLY MOVING / TALKING	① ② ③ ④ ⑤ ⑥ ⑦ ⑧ ⑨ ⑩
STRUGGLING TO SIT STILL	① ② ③ ④ ⑤ ⑥ ⑦ ⑧ ⑨ ⑩
TOUCHING THINGS REPEATEDLY	① ② ③ ④ ⑤ ⑥ ⑦ ⑧ ⑨ ⑩
DIFFICULT SLEEPING	① ② ③ ④ ⑤ ⑥ ⑦ ⑧ ⑨ ⑩

IMPULSIVITY

ACTING WITHOUT THINKING	① ② ③ ④ ⑤ ⑥ ⑦ ⑧ ⑨ ⑩
INTERRUPTING OTHERS	① ② ③ ④ ⑤ ⑥ ⑦ ⑧ ⑨ ⑩
EASILY FRUSTRATED	① ② ③ ④ ⑤ ⑥ ⑦ ⑧ ⑨ ⑩
UNABLE TO HOLD BACK EMOTIONS	① ② ③ ④ ⑤ ⑥ ⑦ ⑧ ⑨ ⑩

MEALS

MEDICATIONS

Water Tracker

NOTES

....
....

<table>
<tr><td>

DAY GOALS

1 ....
2 ....
3 ....

</td><td>

DATE

WEEK

LOCATION

WEIGHT

</td></tr>
</table>

Mood Tracker

BEHAVIOR

INATTENTION

SHORT ATTENTION	① ② ③ ④ ⑤ ⑥ ⑦ ⑧ ⑨ ⑩
UNMOTIVATED / BORED	① ② ③ ④ ⑤ ⑥ ⑦ ⑧ ⑨ ⑩
SHORT ATTENTION	① ② ③ ④ ⑤ ⑥ ⑦ ⑧ ⑨ ⑩
FORGETFUL / CONFUSIONED	① ② ③ ④ ⑤ ⑥ ⑦ ⑧ ⑨ ⑩

HYPERACTIVITY

CONSTANTLY MOVING / TALKING	① ② ③ ④ ⑤ ⑥ ⑦ ⑧ ⑨ ⑩
STRUGGLING TO SIT STILL	① ② ③ ④ ⑤ ⑥ ⑦ ⑧ ⑨ ⑩
TOUCHING THINGS REPEATEDLY	① ② ③ ④ ⑤ ⑥ ⑦ ⑧ ⑨ ⑩
DIFFICULT SLEEPING	① ② ③ ④ ⑤ ⑥ ⑦ ⑧ ⑨ ⑩

IMPULSIVITY

ACTING WITHOUT THINKING	① ② ③ ④ ⑤ ⑥ ⑦ ⑧ ⑨ ⑩
INTERRUPTING OTHERS	① ② ③ ④ ⑤ ⑥ ⑦ ⑧ ⑨ ⑩
EASILY FRUSTRATED	① ② ③ ④ ⑤ ⑥ ⑦ ⑧ ⑨ ⑩
UNABLE TO HOLD BACK EMOTIONS	① ② ③ ④ ⑤ ⑥ ⑦ ⑧ ⑨ ⑩

MEALS	**MEDICATIONS**

Water Tracker

NOTES

....
....

<table>
<tr><td>

DAY GOALS

1 ....
2 ....
3 ....

</td><td>

DATE

WEEK

LOCATION

WEIGHT

</td></tr>
</table>

Mood Tracker

BEHAVIOR

INATTENTION

SHORT ATTENTION	① ② ③ ④ ⑤ ⑥ ⑦ ⑧ ⑨ ⑩
UNMOTIVATED / BORED	① ② ③ ④ ⑤ ⑥ ⑦ ⑧ ⑨ ⑩
SHORT ATTENTION	① ② ③ ④ ⑤ ⑥ ⑦ ⑧ ⑨ ⑩
FORGETFUL / CONFUSIONED	① ② ③ ④ ⑤ ⑥ ⑦ ⑧ ⑨ ⑩

HYPERACTIVITY

CONSTANTLY MOVING / TALKING	① ② ③ ④ ⑤ ⑥ ⑦ ⑧ ⑨ ⑩
STRUGGLING TO SIT STILL	① ② ③ ④ ⑤ ⑥ ⑦ ⑧ ⑨ ⑩
TOUCHING THINGS REPEATEDLY	① ② ③ ④ ⑤ ⑥ ⑦ ⑧ ⑨ ⑩
DIFFICULT SLEEPING	① ② ③ ④ ⑤ ⑥ ⑦ ⑧ ⑨ ⑩

IMPULSIVITY

ACTING WITHOUT THINKING	① ② ③ ④ ⑤ ⑥ ⑦ ⑧ ⑨ ⑩
INTERRUPTING OTHERS	① ② ③ ④ ⑤ ⑥ ⑦ ⑧ ⑨ ⑩
EASILY FRUSTRATED	① ② ③ ④ ⑤ ⑥ ⑦ ⑧ ⑨ ⑩
UNABLE TO HOLD BACK EMOTIONS	① ② ③ ④ ⑤ ⑥ ⑦ ⑧ ⑨ ⑩

MEALS

MEDICATIONS

Water Tracker

NOTES

....
....

<table>
<tr><td>

DAY GOALS

1 ....
2 ....
3 ....

</td><td>

DATE

WEEK

LOCATION

WEIGHT

</td></tr>
</table>

Mood Tracker

BEHAVIOR

INATTENTION

SHORT ATTENTION	① ② ③ ④ ⑤ ⑥ ⑦ ⑧ ⑨ ⑩
UNMOTIVATED / BORED	① ② ③ ④ ⑤ ⑥ ⑦ ⑧ ⑨ ⑩
SHORT ATTENTION	① ② ③ ④ ⑤ ⑥ ⑦ ⑧ ⑨ ⑩
FORGETFUL / CONFUSIONED	① ② ③ ④ ⑤ ⑥ ⑦ ⑧ ⑨ ⑩

HYPERACTIVITY

CONSTANTLY MOVING / TALKING	① ② ③ ④ ⑤ ⑥ ⑦ ⑧ ⑨ ⑩
STRUGGLING TO SIT STILL	① ② ③ ④ ⑤ ⑥ ⑦ ⑧ ⑨ ⑩
TOUCHING THINGS REPEATEDLY	① ② ③ ④ ⑤ ⑥ ⑦ ⑧ ⑨ ⑩
DIFFICULT SLEEPING	① ② ③ ④ ⑤ ⑥ ⑦ ⑧ ⑨ ⑩

IMPULSIVITY

ACTING WITHOUT THINKING	① ② ③ ④ ⑤ ⑥ ⑦ ⑧ ⑨ ⑩
INTERRUPTING OTHERS	① ② ③ ④ ⑤ ⑥ ⑦ ⑧ ⑨ ⑩
EASILY FRUSTRATED	① ② ③ ④ ⑤ ⑥ ⑦ ⑧ ⑨ ⑩
UNABLE TO HOLD BACK EMOTIONS	① ② ③ ④ ⑤ ⑥ ⑦ ⑧ ⑨ ⑩

MEALS	MEDICATIONS

Water Tracker

NOTES

....
....

Mood Tracker

BEHAVIOR

INATTENTION

SHORT ATTENTION	1 2 3 4 5 6 7 8 9 10
UNMOTIVATED / BORED	1 2 3 4 5 6 7 8 9 10
SHORT ATTENTION	1 2 3 4 5 6 7 8 9 10
FORGETFUL / CONFUSIONED	1 2 3 4 5 6 7 8 9 10

HYPERACTIVITY

CONSTANTLY MOVING / TALKING	1 2 3 4 5 6 7 8 9 10
STRUGGLING TO SIT STILL	1 2 3 4 5 6 7 8 9 10
TOUCHING THINGS REPEATEDLY	1 2 3 4 5 6 7 8 9 10
DIFFICULT SLEEPING	1 2 3 4 5 6 7 8 9 10

IMPULSIVITY

ACTING WITHOUT THINKING	1 2 3 4 5 6 7 8 9 10
INTERRUPTING OTHERS	1 2 3 4 5 6 7 8 9 10
EASILY FRUSTRATED	1 2 3 4 5 6 7 8 9 10
UNABLE TO HOLD BACK EMOTIONS	1 2 3 4 5 6 7 8 9 10

MEALS

MEDICATIONS

Water Tracker

NOTES

....
....

<table>
<tr><td>

DAY GOALS

1 ....

2 ....

3 ....

</td><td>

DATE

WEEK

LOCATION

WEIGHT

</td></tr>
</table>

Mood Tracker

BEHAVIOR

INATTENTION

SHORT ATTENTION	① ② ③ ④ ⑤ ⑥ ⑦ ⑧ ⑨ ⑩
UNMOTIVATED / BORED	① ② ③ ④ ⑤ ⑥ ⑦ ⑧ ⑨ ⑩
SHORT ATTENTION	① ② ③ ④ ⑤ ⑥ ⑦ ⑧ ⑨ ⑩
FORGETFUL / CONFUSIONED	① ② ③ ④ ⑤ ⑥ ⑦ ⑧ ⑨ ⑩

HYPERACTIVITY

CONSTANTLY MOVING / TALKING	① ② ③ ④ ⑤ ⑥ ⑦ ⑧ ⑨ ⑩
STRUGGLING TO SIT STILL	① ② ③ ④ ⑤ ⑥ ⑦ ⑧ ⑨ ⑩
TOUCHING THINGS REPEATEDLY	① ② ③ ④ ⑤ ⑥ ⑦ ⑧ ⑨ ⑩
DIFFICULT SLEEPING	① ② ③ ④ ⑤ ⑥ ⑦ ⑧ ⑨ ⑩

IMPULSIVITY

ACTING WITHOUT THINKING	① ② ③ ④ ⑤ ⑥ ⑦ ⑧ ⑨ ⑩
INTERRUPTING OTHERS	① ② ③ ④ ⑤ ⑥ ⑦ ⑧ ⑨ ⑩
EASILY FRUSTRATED	① ② ③ ④ ⑤ ⑥ ⑦ ⑧ ⑨ ⑩
UNABLE TO HOLD BACK EMOTIONS	① ② ③ ④ ⑤ ⑥ ⑦ ⑧ ⑨ ⑩

MEALS	MEDICATIONS

Water Tracker

NOTES

....

....

<table>
<tr><td>

DAY GOALS

1 ....
2 ....
3 ....

</td><td>

DATE

WEEK

LOCATION

WEIGHT

</td></tr>
</table>

Mood Tracker 😦 😐 😣 😢 😠 😀

BEHAVIOR

INATTENTION

SHORT ATTENTION	① ② ③ ④ ⑤ ⑥ ⑦ ⑧ ⑨ ⑩
UNMOTIVATED / BORED	① ② ③ ④ ⑤ ⑥ ⑦ ⑧ ⑨ ⑩
SHORT ATTENTION	① ② ③ ④ ⑤ ⑥ ⑦ ⑧ ⑨ ⑩
FORGETFUL / CONFUSIONED	① ② ③ ④ ⑤ ⑥ ⑦ ⑧ ⑨ ⑩

HYPERACTIVITY

CONSTANTLY MOVING / TALKING	① ② ③ ④ ⑤ ⑥ ⑦ ⑧ ⑨ ⑩
STRUGGLING TO SIT STILL	① ② ③ ④ ⑤ ⑥ ⑦ ⑧ ⑨ ⑩
TOUCHING THINGS REPEATEDLY	① ② ③ ④ ⑤ ⑥ ⑦ ⑧ ⑨ ⑩
DIFFICULT SLEEPING	① ② ③ ④ ⑤ ⑥ ⑦ ⑧ ⑨ ⑩

IMPULSIVITY

ACTING WITHOUT THINKING	① ② ③ ④ ⑤ ⑥ ⑦ ⑧ ⑨ ⑩
INTERRUPTING OTHERS	① ② ③ ④ ⑤ ⑥ ⑦ ⑧ ⑨ ⑩
EASILY FRUSTRATED	① ② ③ ④ ⑤ ⑥ ⑦ ⑧ ⑨ ⑩
UNABLE TO HOLD BACK EMOTIONS	① ② ③ ④ ⑤ ⑥ ⑦ ⑧ ⑨ ⑩

MEALS	MEDICATIONS

Water Tracker 🍼 🍼 🍼 🍼 🍼 🍼 🍼 🍼

NOTES

....
....

<table>
<tr><td>

DAY GOALS

1 ....
2 ....
3 ....

</td><td>

DATE

WEEK

LOCATION

WEIGHT

</td></tr>
</table>

Mood Tracker

BEHAVIOR

INATTENTION

SHORT ATTENTION	① ② ③ ④ ⑤ ⑥ ⑦ ⑧ ⑨ ⑩
UNMOTIVATED / BORED	① ② ③ ④ ⑤ ⑥ ⑦ ⑧ ⑨ ⑩
SHORT ATTENTION	① ② ③ ④ ⑤ ⑥ ⑦ ⑧ ⑨ ⑩
FORGETFUL / CONFUSIONED	① ② ③ ④ ⑤ ⑥ ⑦ ⑧ ⑨ ⑩

HYPERACTIVITY

CONSTANTLY MOVING / TALKING	① ② ③ ④ ⑤ ⑥ ⑦ ⑧ ⑨ ⑩
STRUGGLING TO SIT STILL	① ② ③ ④ ⑤ ⑥ ⑦ ⑧ ⑨ ⑩
TOUCHING THINGS REPEATEDLY	① ② ③ ④ ⑤ ⑥ ⑦ ⑧ ⑨ ⑩
DIFFICULT SLEEPING	① ② ③ ④ ⑤ ⑥ ⑦ ⑧ ⑨ ⑩

IMPULSIVITY

ACTING WITHOUT THINKING	① ② ③ ④ ⑤ ⑥ ⑦ ⑧ ⑨ ⑩
INTERRUPTING OTHERS	① ② ③ ④ ⑤ ⑥ ⑦ ⑧ ⑨ ⑩
EASILY FRUSTRATED	① ② ③ ④ ⑤ ⑥ ⑦ ⑧ ⑨ ⑩
UNABLE TO HOLD BACK EMOTIONS	① ② ③ ④ ⑤ ⑥ ⑦ ⑧ ⑨ ⑩

MEALS

MEDICATIONS

Water Tracker

NOTES

....
....

<table>
<tr><td>

DAY GOALS

1 ....
2 ....
3 ....

</td><td>

DATE

WEEK

LOCATION

WEIGHT

</td></tr>
</table>

Mood Tracker ☹ 😐 😣 😢 😠 😃

BEHAVIOR

INATTENTION

SHORT ATTENTION	① ② ③ ④ ⑤ ⑥ ⑦ ⑧ ⑨ ⑩
UNMOTIVATED / BORED	① ② ③ ④ ⑤ ⑥ ⑦ ⑧ ⑨ ⑩
SHORT ATTENTION	① ② ③ ④ ⑤ ⑥ ⑦ ⑧ ⑨ ⑩
FORGETFUL / CONFUSIONED	① ② ③ ④ ⑤ ⑥ ⑦ ⑧ ⑨ ⑩

HYPERACTIVITY

CONSTANTLY MOVING / TALKING	① ② ③ ④ ⑤ ⑥ ⑦ ⑧ ⑨ ⑩
STRUGGLING TO SIT STILL	① ② ③ ④ ⑤ ⑥ ⑦ ⑧ ⑨ ⑩
TOUCHING THINGS REPEATEDLY	① ② ③ ④ ⑤ ⑥ ⑦ ⑧ ⑨ ⑩
DIFFICULT SLEEPING	① ② ③ ④ ⑤ ⑥ ⑦ ⑧ ⑨ ⑩

IMPULSIVITY

ACTING WITHOUT THINKING	① ② ③ ④ ⑤ ⑥ ⑦ ⑧ ⑨ ⑩
INTERRUPTING OTHERS	① ② ③ ④ ⑤ ⑥ ⑦ ⑧ ⑨ ⑩
EASILY FRUSTRATED	① ② ③ ④ ⑤ ⑥ ⑦ ⑧ ⑨ ⑩
UNABLE TO HOLD BACK EMOTIONS	① ② ③ ④ ⑤ ⑥ ⑦ ⑧ ⑨ ⑩

MEALS

MEDICATIONS

Water Tracker 🍼 🍼 🍼 🍼 🍼 🍼 🍼 🍼

NOTES

....

....

DAY GOALS	
1	....
2	....
3	....

DATE
WEEK
LOCATION
WEIGHT

Mood Tracker

BEHAVIOR

INATTENTION

SHORT ATTENTION	1 2 3 4 5 6 7 8 9 10
UNMOTIVATED / BORED	1 2 3 4 5 6 7 8 9 10
SHORT ATTENTION	1 2 3 4 5 6 7 8 9 10
FORGETFUL / CONFUSIONED	1 2 3 4 5 6 7 8 9 10

HYPERACTIVITY

CONSTANTLY MOVING / TALKING	1 2 3 4 5 6 7 8 9 10
STRUGGLING TO SIT STILL	1 2 3 4 5 6 7 8 9 10
TOUCHING THINGS REPEATEDLY	1 2 3 4 5 6 7 8 9 10
DIFFICULT SLEEPING	1 2 3 4 5 6 7 8 9 10

IMPULSIVITY

ACTING WITHOUT THINKING	1 2 3 4 5 6 7 8 9 10
INTERRUPTING OTHERS	1 2 3 4 5 6 7 8 9 10
EASILY FRUSTRATED	1 2 3 4 5 6 7 8 9 10
UNABLE TO HOLD BACK EMOTIONS	1 2 3 4 5 6 7 8 9 10

MEALS

MEDICATIONS

Water Tracker

NOTES

....

....

<table>
<tr><td>

DAY GOALS

1 ....
2 ....
3 ....

</td><td>

DATE

WEEK

LOCATION

WEIGHT

</td></tr>
</table>

Mood Tracker

BEHAVIOR

INATTENTION

SHORT ATTENTION	① ② ③ ④ ⑤ ⑥ ⑦ ⑧ ⑨ ⑩
UNMOTIVATED / BORED	① ② ③ ④ ⑤ ⑥ ⑦ ⑧ ⑨ ⑩
SHORT ATTENTION	① ② ③ ④ ⑤ ⑥ ⑦ ⑧ ⑨ ⑩
FORGETFUL / CONFUSIONED	① ② ③ ④ ⑤ ⑥ ⑦ ⑧ ⑨ ⑩

HYPERACTIVITY

CONSTANTLY MOVING / TALKING	① ② ③ ④ ⑤ ⑥ ⑦ ⑧ ⑨ ⑩
STRUGGLING TO SIT STILL	① ② ③ ④ ⑤ ⑥ ⑦ ⑧ ⑨ ⑩
TOUCHING THINGS REPEATEDLY	① ② ③ ④ ⑤ ⑥ ⑦ ⑧ ⑨ ⑩
DIFFICULT SLEEPING	① ② ③ ④ ⑤ ⑥ ⑦ ⑧ ⑨ ⑩

IMPULSIVITY

ACTING WITHOUT THINKING	① ② ③ ④ ⑤ ⑥ ⑦ ⑧ ⑨ ⑩
INTERRUPTING OTHERS	① ② ③ ④ ⑤ ⑥ ⑦ ⑧ ⑨ ⑩
EASILY FRUSTRATED	① ② ③ ④ ⑤ ⑥ ⑦ ⑧ ⑨ ⑩
UNABLE TO HOLD BACK EMOTIONS	① ② ③ ④ ⑤ ⑥ ⑦ ⑧ ⑨ ⑩

MEALS

MEDICATIONS

Water Tracker

NOTES

....
....

<table>
<tr><td>

DAY GOALS

1 ....
2 ....
3 ....

</td><td>

DATE

WEEK

LOCATION

WEIGHT

</td></tr>
</table>

Mood Tracker

BEHAVIOR

INATTENTION

SHORT ATTENTION	① ② ③ ④ ⑤ ⑥ ⑦ ⑧ ⑨ ⑩
UNMOTIVATED / BORED	① ② ③ ④ ⑤ ⑥ ⑦ ⑧ ⑨ ⑩
SHORT ATTENTION	① ② ③ ④ ⑤ ⑥ ⑦ ⑧ ⑨ ⑩
FORGETFUL / CONFUSIONED	① ② ③ ④ ⑤ ⑥ ⑦ ⑧ ⑨ ⑩

HYPERACTIVITY

CONSTANTLY MOVING / TALKING	① ② ③ ④ ⑤ ⑥ ⑦ ⑧ ⑨ ⑩
STRUGGLING TO SIT STILL	① ② ③ ④ ⑤ ⑥ ⑦ ⑧ ⑨ ⑩
TOUCHING THINGS REPEATEDLY	① ② ③ ④ ⑤ ⑥ ⑦ ⑧ ⑨ ⑩
DIFFICULT SLEEPING	① ② ③ ④ ⑤ ⑥ ⑦ ⑧ ⑨ ⑩

IMPULSIVITY

ACTING WITHOUT THINKING	① ② ③ ④ ⑤ ⑥ ⑦ ⑧ ⑨ ⑩
INTERRUPTING OTHERS	① ② ③ ④ ⑤ ⑥ ⑦ ⑧ ⑨ ⑩
EASILY FRUSTRATED	① ② ③ ④ ⑤ ⑥ ⑦ ⑧ ⑨ ⑩
UNABLE TO HOLD BACK EMOTIONS	① ② ③ ④ ⑤ ⑥ ⑦ ⑧ ⑨ ⑩

MEALS

MEDICATIONS

Water Tracker

NOTES

....
....

<table>
<tr><td>

DAY GOALS

1 ....
2 ....
3 ....

</td><td>

DATE

WEEK

LOCATION

WEIGHT

</td></tr>
</table>

Mood Tracker

BEHAVIOR

INATTENTION

SHORT ATTENTION	① ② ③ ④ ⑤ ⑥ ⑦ ⑧ ⑨ ⑩
UNMOTIVATED / BORED	① ② ③ ④ ⑤ ⑥ ⑦ ⑧ ⑨ ⑩
SHORT ATTENTION	① ② ③ ④ ⑤ ⑥ ⑦ ⑧ ⑨ ⑩
FORGETFUL / CONFUSIONED	① ② ③ ④ ⑤ ⑥ ⑦ ⑧ ⑨ ⑩

HYPERACTIVITY

CONSTANTLY MOVING / TALKING	① ② ③ ④ ⑤ ⑥ ⑦ ⑧ ⑨ ⑩
STRUGGLING TO SIT STILL	① ② ③ ④ ⑤ ⑥ ⑦ ⑧ ⑨ ⑩
TOUCHING THINGS REPEATEDLY	① ② ③ ④ ⑤ ⑥ ⑦ ⑧ ⑨ ⑩
DIFFICULT SLEEPING	① ② ③ ④ ⑤ ⑥ ⑦ ⑧ ⑨ ⑩

IMPULSIVITY

ACTING WITHOUT THINKING	① ② ③ ④ ⑤ ⑥ ⑦ ⑧ ⑨ ⑩
INTERRUPTING OTHERS	① ② ③ ④ ⑤ ⑥ ⑦ ⑧ ⑨ ⑩
EASILY FRUSTRATED	① ② ③ ④ ⑤ ⑥ ⑦ ⑧ ⑨ ⑩
UNABLE TO HOLD BACK EMOTIONS	① ② ③ ④ ⑤ ⑥ ⑦ ⑧ ⑨ ⑩

MEALS	MEDICATIONS

Water Tracker

NOTES

....
....

<table>
<tr><td>

DAY GOALS

1 ....
2 ....
3 ....

</td><td>

DATE

WEEK

LOCATION

WEIGHT

</td></tr>
</table>

Mood Tracker

BEHAVIOR

INATTENTION

SHORT ATTENTION	① ② ③ ④ ⑤ ⑥ ⑦ ⑧ ⑨ ⑩
UNMOTIVATED / BORED	① ② ③ ④ ⑤ ⑥ ⑦ ⑧ ⑨ ⑩
SHORT ATTENTION	① ② ③ ④ ⑤ ⑥ ⑦ ⑧ ⑨ ⑩
FORGETFUL / CONFUSIONED	① ② ③ ④ ⑤ ⑥ ⑦ ⑧ ⑨ ⑩

HYPERACTIVITY

CONSTANTLY MOVING / TALKING	① ② ③ ④ ⑤ ⑥ ⑦ ⑧ ⑨ ⑩
STRUGGLING TO SIT STILL	① ② ③ ④ ⑤ ⑥ ⑦ ⑧ ⑨ ⑩
TOUCHING THINGS REPEATEDLY	① ② ③ ④ ⑤ ⑥ ⑦ ⑧ ⑨ ⑩
DIFFICULT SLEEPING	① ② ③ ④ ⑤ ⑥ ⑦ ⑧ ⑨ ⑩

IMPULSIVITY

ACTING WITHOUT THINKING	① ② ③ ④ ⑤ ⑥ ⑦ ⑧ ⑨ ⑩
INTERRUPTING OTHERS	① ② ③ ④ ⑤ ⑥ ⑦ ⑧ ⑨ ⑩
EASILY FRUSTRATED	① ② ③ ④ ⑤ ⑥ ⑦ ⑧ ⑨ ⑩
UNABLE TO HOLD BACK EMOTIONS	① ② ③ ④ ⑤ ⑥ ⑦ ⑧ ⑨ ⑩

MEALS	MEDICATIONS

Water Tracker

NOTES

....
....

<table><tr><td>

DAY GOALS

1 ....
2 ....
3 ....

</td><td>

DATE

WEEK

LOCATION

WEIGHT

</td></tr></table>

Mood Tracker

BEHAVIOR

INATTENTION

SHORT ATTENTION	① ② ③ ④ ⑤ ⑥ ⑦ ⑧ ⑨ ⑩
UNMOTIVATED / BORED	① ② ③ ④ ⑤ ⑥ ⑦ ⑧ ⑨ ⑩
SHORT ATTENTION	① ② ③ ④ ⑤ ⑥ ⑦ ⑧ ⑨ ⑩
FORGETFUL / CONFUSIONED	① ② ③ ④ ⑤ ⑥ ⑦ ⑧ ⑨ ⑩

HYPERACTIVITY

CONSTANTLY MOVING / TALKING	① ② ③ ④ ⑤ ⑥ ⑦ ⑧ ⑨ ⑩
STRUGGLING TO SIT STILL	① ② ③ ④ ⑤ ⑥ ⑦ ⑧ ⑨ ⑩
TOUCHING THINGS REPEATEDLY	① ② ③ ④ ⑤ ⑥ ⑦ ⑧ ⑨ ⑩
DIFFICULT SLEEPING	① ② ③ ④ ⑤ ⑥ ⑦ ⑧ ⑨ ⑩

IMPULSIVITY

ACTING WITHOUT THINKING	① ② ③ ④ ⑤ ⑥ ⑦ ⑧ ⑨ ⑩
INTERRUPTING OTHERS	① ② ③ ④ ⑤ ⑥ ⑦ ⑧ ⑨ ⑩
EASILY FRUSTRATED	① ② ③ ④ ⑤ ⑥ ⑦ ⑧ ⑨ ⑩
UNABLE TO HOLD BACK EMOTIONS	① ② ③ ④ ⑤ ⑥ ⑦ ⑧ ⑨ ⑩

MEALS

MEDICATIONS

Water Tracker

NOTES

....
....

<table>
<tr><td>

DAY GOALS

1 ....
2 ....
3 ....

</td><td>

DATE

WEEK

LOCATION

WEIGHT

</td></tr>
</table>

Mood Tracker

BEHAVIOR

INATTENTION

SHORT ATTENTION	① ② ③ ④ ⑤ ⑥ ⑦ ⑧ ⑨ ⑩
UNMOTIVATED / BORED	① ② ③ ④ ⑤ ⑥ ⑦ ⑧ ⑨ ⑩
SHORT ATTENTION	① ② ③ ④ ⑤ ⑥ ⑦ ⑧ ⑨ ⑩
FORGETFUL / CONFUSIONED	① ② ③ ④ ⑤ ⑥ ⑦ ⑧ ⑨ ⑩

HYPERACTIVITY

CONSTANTLY MOVING / TALKING	① ② ③ ④ ⑤ ⑥ ⑦ ⑧ ⑨ ⑩
STRUGGLING TO SIT STILL	① ② ③ ④ ⑤ ⑥ ⑦ ⑧ ⑨ ⑩
TOUCHING THINGS REPEATEDLY	① ② ③ ④ ⑤ ⑥ ⑦ ⑧ ⑨ ⑩
DIFFICULT SLEEPING	① ② ③ ④ ⑤ ⑥ ⑦ ⑧ ⑨ ⑩

IMPULSIVITY

ACTING WITHOUT THINKING	① ② ③ ④ ⑤ ⑥ ⑦ ⑧ ⑨ ⑩
INTERRUPTING OTHERS	① ② ③ ④ ⑤ ⑥ ⑦ ⑧ ⑨ ⑩
EASILY FRUSTRATED	① ② ③ ④ ⑤ ⑥ ⑦ ⑧ ⑨ ⑩
UNABLE TO HOLD BACK EMOTIONS	① ② ③ ④ ⑤ ⑥ ⑦ ⑧ ⑨ ⑩

MEALS

MEDICATIONS

Water Tracker

NOTES

....

....

DAY GOALS

1 ....
2 ....
3 ....

DATE

WEEK

LOCATION

WEIGHT

Mood Tracker

BEHAVIOR

INATTENTION

SHORT ATTENTION	1 2 3 4 5 6 7 8 9 10
UNMOTIVATED / BORED	1 2 3 4 5 6 7 8 9 10
SHORT ATTENTION	1 2 3 4 5 6 7 8 9 10
FORGETFUL / CONFUSIONED	1 2 3 4 5 6 7 8 9 10

HYPERACTIVITY

CONSTANTLY MOVING / TALKING	1 2 3 4 5 6 7 8 9 10
STRUGGLING TO SIT STILL	1 2 3 4 5 6 7 8 9 10
TOUCHING THINGS REPEATEDLY	1 2 3 4 5 6 7 8 9 10
DIFFICULT SLEEPING	1 2 3 4 5 6 7 8 9 10

IMPULSIVITY

ACTING WITHOUT THINKING	1 2 3 4 5 6 7 8 9 10
INTERRUPTING OTHERS	1 2 3 4 5 6 7 8 9 10
EASILY FRUSTRATED	1 2 3 4 5 6 7 8 9 10
UNABLE TO HOLD BACK EMOTIONS	1 2 3 4 5 6 7 8 9 10

MEALS

MEDICATIONS

Water Tracker

NOTES

....
....

<table>
<tr><td>DAY GOALS</td><td>DATE</td></tr>
<tr><td>1 ....
2 ....
3 ....</td><td>WEEK

LOCATION

WEIGHT</td></tr>
</table>

Mood Tracker

BEHAVIOR

INATTENTION

SHORT ATTENTION	1 2 3 4 5 6 7 8 9 10
UNMOTIVATED / BORED	1 2 3 4 5 6 7 8 9 10
SHORT ATTENTION	1 2 3 4 5 6 7 8 9 10
FORGETFUL / CONFUSIONED	1 2 3 4 5 6 7 8 9 10

HYPERACTIVITY

CONSTANTLY MOVING / TALKING	1 2 3 4 5 6 7 8 9 10
STRUGGLING TO SIT STILL	1 2 3 4 5 6 7 8 9 10
TOUCHING THINGS REPEATEDLY	1 2 3 4 5 6 7 8 9 10
DIFFICULT SLEEPING	1 2 3 4 5 6 7 8 9 10

IMPULSIVITY

ACTING WITHOUT THINKING	1 2 3 4 5 6 7 8 9 10
INTERRUPTING OTHERS	1 2 3 4 5 6 7 8 9 10
EASILY FRUSTRATED	1 2 3 4 5 6 7 8 9 10
UNABLE TO HOLD BACK EMOTIONS	1 2 3 4 5 6 7 8 9 10

MEALS

MEDICATIONS

Water Tracker

NOTES

....
....

<table>
<tr><td>

DAY GOALS

1 ....
2 ....
3 ....

</td><td>

DATE

WEEK

LOCATION

WEIGHT

</td></tr>
</table>

Mood Tracker

BEHAVIOR

INATTENTION

SHORT ATTENTION	① ② ③ ④ ⑤ ⑥ ⑦ ⑧ ⑨ ⑩
UNMOTIVATED / BORED	① ② ③ ④ ⑤ ⑥ ⑦ ⑧ ⑨ ⑩
SHORT ATTENTION	① ② ③ ④ ⑤ ⑥ ⑦ ⑧ ⑨ ⑩
FORGETFUL / CONFUSIONED	① ② ③ ④ ⑤ ⑥ ⑦ ⑧ ⑨ ⑩

HYPERACTIVITY

CONSTANTLY MOVING / TALKING	① ② ③ ④ ⑤ ⑥ ⑦ ⑧ ⑨ ⑩
STRUGGLING TO SIT STILL	① ② ③ ④ ⑤ ⑥ ⑦ ⑧ ⑨ ⑩
TOUCHING THINGS REPEATEDLY	① ② ③ ④ ⑤ ⑥ ⑦ ⑧ ⑨ ⑩
DIFFICULT SLEEPING	① ② ③ ④ ⑤ ⑥ ⑦ ⑧ ⑨ ⑩

IMPULSIVITY

ACTING WITHOUT THINKING	① ② ③ ④ ⑤ ⑥ ⑦ ⑧ ⑨ ⑩
INTERRUPTING OTHERS	① ② ③ ④ ⑤ ⑥ ⑦ ⑧ ⑨ ⑩
EASILY FRUSTRATED	① ② ③ ④ ⑤ ⑥ ⑦ ⑧ ⑨ ⑩
UNABLE TO HOLD BACK EMOTIONS	① ② ③ ④ ⑤ ⑥ ⑦ ⑧ ⑨ ⑩

MEALS	MEDICATIONS

Water Tracker

NOTES

....
....

DATE

WEEK

LOCATION

WEIGHT

Mood Tracker

INATTENTION

SHORT ATTENTION	① ② ③ ④ ⑤ ⑥ ⑦ ⑧ ⑨ ⑩
UNMOTIVATED / BORED	① ② ③ ④ ⑤ ⑥ ⑦ ⑧ ⑨ ⑩
SHORT ATTENTION	① ② ③ ④ ⑤ ⑥ ⑦ ⑧ ⑨ ⑩
FORGETFUL / CONFUSIONED	① ② ③ ④ ⑤ ⑥ ⑦ ⑧ ⑨ ⑩

HYPERACTIVITY

CONSTANTLY MOVING / TALKING	① ② ③ ④ ⑤ ⑥ ⑦ ⑧ ⑨ ⑩
STRUGGLING TO SIT STILL	① ② ③ ④ ⑤ ⑥ ⑦ ⑧ ⑨ ⑩
TOUCHING THINGS REPEATEDLY	① ② ③ ④ ⑤ ⑥ ⑦ ⑧ ⑨ ⑩
DIFFICULT SLEEPING	① ② ③ ④ ⑤ ⑥ ⑦ ⑧ ⑨ ⑩

IMPULSIVITY

ACTING WITHOUT THINKING	① ② ③ ④ ⑤ ⑥ ⑦ ⑧ ⑨ ⑩
INTERRUPTING OTHERS	① ② ③ ④ ⑤ ⑥ ⑦ ⑧ ⑨ ⑩
EASILY FRUSTRATED	① ② ③ ④ ⑤ ⑥ ⑦ ⑧ ⑨ ⑩
UNABLE TO HOLD BACK EMOTIONS	① ② ③ ④ ⑤ ⑥ ⑦ ⑧ ⑨ ⑩

MEALS

MEDICATIONS

Water Tracker

<table>
<tr><td>

DAY GOALS

1 ....
2 ....
3 ....

</td><td>

DATE

WEEK

LOCATION

WEIGHT

</td></tr>
</table>

Mood Tracker 😦 😐 😖 😢 😠 😃

BEHAVIOR

INATTENTION

SHORT ATTENTION	① ② ③ ④ ⑤ ⑥ ⑦ ⑧ ⑨ ⑩
UNMOTIVATED / BORED	① ② ③ ④ ⑤ ⑥ ⑦ ⑧ ⑨ ⑩
SHORT ATTENTION	① ② ③ ④ ⑤ ⑥ ⑦ ⑧ ⑨ ⑩
FORGETFUL / CONFUSIONED	① ② ③ ④ ⑤ ⑥ ⑦ ⑧ ⑨ ⑩

HYPERACTIVITY

CONSTANTLY MOVING / TALKING	① ② ③ ④ ⑤ ⑥ ⑦ ⑧ ⑨ ⑩
STRUGGLING TO SIT STILL	① ② ③ ④ ⑤ ⑥ ⑦ ⑧ ⑨ ⑩
TOUCHING THINGS REPEATEDLY	① ② ③ ④ ⑤ ⑥ ⑦ ⑧ ⑨ ⑩
DIFFICULT SLEEPING	① ② ③ ④ ⑤ ⑥ ⑦ ⑧ ⑨ ⑩

IMPULSIVITY

ACTING WITHOUT THINKING	① ② ③ ④ ⑤ ⑥ ⑦ ⑧ ⑨ ⑩
INTERRUPTING OTHERS	① ② ③ ④ ⑤ ⑥ ⑦ ⑧ ⑨ ⑩
EASILY FRUSTRATED	① ② ③ ④ ⑤ ⑥ ⑦ ⑧ ⑨ ⑩
UNABLE TO HOLD BACK EMOTIONS	① ② ③ ④ ⑤ ⑥ ⑦ ⑧ ⑨ ⑩

MEALS

MEDICATIONS

Water Tracker

NOTES

....
....

DATE

WEEK

LOCATION

WEIGHT

Mood Tracker

BEHAVIOR

INATTENTION

SHORT ATTENTION	1 2 3 4 5 6 7 8 9 10
UNMOTIVATED / BORED	1 2 3 4 5 6 7 8 9 10
SHORT ATTENTION	1 2 3 4 5 6 7 8 9 10
FORGETFUL / CONFUSIONED	1 2 3 4 5 6 7 8 9 10

HYPERACTIVITY

CONSTANTLY MOVING / TALKING	1 2 3 4 5 6 7 8 9 10
STRUGGLING TO SIT STILL	1 2 3 4 5 6 7 8 9 10
TOUCHING THINGS REPEATEDLY	1 2 3 4 5 6 7 8 9 10
DIFFICULT SLEEPING	1 2 3 4 5 6 7 8 9 10

IMPULSIVITY

ACTING WITHOUT THINKING	1 2 3 4 5 6 7 8 9 10
INTERRUPTING OTHERS	1 2 3 4 5 6 7 8 9 10
EASILY FRUSTRATED	1 2 3 4 5 6 7 8 9 10
UNABLE TO HOLD BACK EMOTIONS	1 2 3 4 5 6 7 8 9 10

MEALS

MEDICATIONS

Water Tracker

NOTES

DATE

WEEK

LOCATION

WEIGHT

Mood Tracker

BEHAVIOR

INATTENTION

SHORT ATTENTION	1 2 3 4 5 6 7 8 9 10
UNMOTIVATED / BORED	1 2 3 4 5 6 7 8 9 10
SHORT ATTENTION	1 2 3 4 5 6 7 8 9 10
FORGETFUL / CONFUSIONED	1 2 3 4 5 6 7 8 9 10

HYPERACTIVITY

CONSTANTLY MOVING / TALKING	1 2 3 4 5 6 7 8 9 10
STRUGGLING TO SIT STILL	1 2 3 4 5 6 7 8 9 10
TOUCHING THINGS REPEATEDLY	1 2 3 4 5 6 7 8 9 10
DIFFICULT SLEEPING	1 2 3 4 5 6 7 8 9 10

IMPULSIVITY

ACTING WITHOUT THINKING	1 2 3 4 5 6 7 8 9 10
INTERRUPTING OTHERS	1 2 3 4 5 6 7 8 9 10
EASILY FRUSTRATED	1 2 3 4 5 6 7 8 9 10
UNABLE TO HOLD BACK EMOTIONS	1 2 3 4 5 6 7 8 9 10

MEALS

MEDICATIONS

Water Tracker

NOTES

Mood Tracker

INATTENTION

SHORT ATTENTION	① ② ③ ④ ⑤ ⑥ ⑦ ⑧ ⑨ ⑩
UNMOTIVATED / BORED	① ② ③ ④ ⑤ ⑥ ⑦ ⑧ ⑨ ⑩
SHORT ATTENTION	① ② ③ ④ ⑤ ⑥ ⑦ ⑧ ⑨ ⑩
FORGETFUL / CONFUSIONED	① ② ③ ④ ⑤ ⑥ ⑦ ⑧ ⑨ ⑩

HYPERACTIVITY

CONSTANTLY MOVING / TALKING	① ② ③ ④ ⑤ ⑥ ⑦ ⑧ ⑨ ⑩
STRUGGLING TO SIT STILL	① ② ③ ④ ⑤ ⑥ ⑦ ⑧ ⑨ ⑩
TOUCHING THINGS REPEATEDLY	① ② ③ ④ ⑤ ⑥ ⑦ ⑧ ⑨ ⑩
DIFFICULT SLEEPING	① ② ③ ④ ⑤ ⑥ ⑦ ⑧ ⑨ ⑩

IMPULSIVITY

ACTING WITHOUT THINKING	① ② ③ ④ ⑤ ⑥ ⑦ ⑧ ⑨ ⑩
INTERRUPTING OTHERS	① ② ③ ④ ⑤ ⑥ ⑦ ⑧ ⑨ ⑩
EASILY FRUSTRATED	① ② ③ ④ ⑤ ⑥ ⑦ ⑧ ⑨ ⑩
UNABLE TO HOLD BACK EMOTIONS	① ② ③ ④ ⑤ ⑥ ⑦ ⑧ ⑨ ⑩

MEALS

MEDICATIONS

Water Tracker

<table>
<tr><td>

DAY GOALS

1 ....
2 ....
3 ....

</td><td>

DATE

WEEK

LOCATION

WEIGHT

</td></tr>
</table>

Mood Tracker

BEHAVIOR

INATTENTION

SHORT ATTENTION	① ② ③ ④ ⑤ ⑥ ⑦ ⑧ ⑨ ⑩
UNMOTIVATED / BORED	① ② ③ ④ ⑤ ⑥ ⑦ ⑧ ⑨ ⑩
SHORT ATTENTION	① ② ③ ④ ⑤ ⑥ ⑦ ⑧ ⑨ ⑩
FORGETFUL / CONFUSIONED	① ② ③ ④ ⑤ ⑥ ⑦ ⑧ ⑨ ⑩

HYPERACTIVITY

CONSTANTLY MOVING / TALKING	① ② ③ ④ ⑤ ⑥ ⑦ ⑧ ⑨ ⑩
STRUGGLING TO SIT STILL	① ② ③ ④ ⑤ ⑥ ⑦ ⑧ ⑨ ⑩
TOUCHING THINGS REPEATEDLY	① ② ③ ④ ⑤ ⑥ ⑦ ⑧ ⑨ ⑩
DIFFICULT SLEEPING	① ② ③ ④ ⑤ ⑥ ⑦ ⑧ ⑨ ⑩

IMPULSIVITY

ACTING WITHOUT THINKING	① ② ③ ④ ⑤ ⑥ ⑦ ⑧ ⑨ ⑩
INTERRUPTING OTHERS	① ② ③ ④ ⑤ ⑥ ⑦ ⑧ ⑨ ⑩
EASILY FRUSTRATED	① ② ③ ④ ⑤ ⑥ ⑦ ⑧ ⑨ ⑩
UNABLE TO HOLD BACK EMOTIONS	① ② ③ ④ ⑤ ⑥ ⑦ ⑧ ⑨ ⑩

MEALS	MEDICATIONS

Water Tracker

NOTES

....
....

DATE
WEEK
LOCATION
WEIGHT

Mood Tracker

BEHAVIOR

INATTENTION

SHORT ATTENTION	① ② ③ ④ ⑤ ⑥ ⑦ ⑧ ⑨ ⑩
UNMOTIVATED / BORED	① ② ③ ④ ⑤ ⑥ ⑦ ⑧ ⑨ ⑩
SHORT ATTENTION	① ② ③ ④ ⑤ ⑥ ⑦ ⑧ ⑨ ⑩
FORGETFUL / CONFUSIONED	① ② ③ ④ ⑤ ⑥ ⑦ ⑧ ⑨ ⑩

HYPERACTIVITY

CONSTANTLY MOVING / TALKING	① ② ③ ④ ⑤ ⑥ ⑦ ⑧ ⑨ ⑩
STRUGGLING TO SIT STILL	① ② ③ ④ ⑤ ⑥ ⑦ ⑧ ⑨ ⑩
TOUCHING THINGS REPEATEDLY	① ② ③ ④ ⑤ ⑥ ⑦ ⑧ ⑨ ⑩
DIFFICULT SLEEPING	① ② ③ ④ ⑤ ⑥ ⑦ ⑧ ⑨ ⑩

IMPULSIVITY

ACTING WITHOUT THINKING	① ② ③ ④ ⑤ ⑥ ⑦ ⑧ ⑨ ⑩
INTERRUPTING OTHERS	① ② ③ ④ ⑤ ⑥ ⑦ ⑧ ⑨ ⑩
EASILY FRUSTRATED	① ② ③ ④ ⑤ ⑥ ⑦ ⑧ ⑨ ⑩
UNABLE TO HOLD BACK EMOTIONS	① ② ③ ④ ⑤ ⑥ ⑦ ⑧ ⑨ ⑩

MEALS

MEDICATIONS

Water Tracker

NOTES

<table>
<tr><td>

DAY GOALS

1 ....
2 ....
3 ....

</td><td>

DATE

WEEK

LOCATION

WEIGHT

</td></tr>
</table>

Mood Tracker

BEHAVIOR

INATTENTION

SHORT ATTENTION	① ② ③ ④ ⑤ ⑥ ⑦ ⑧ ⑨ ⑩
UNMOTIVATED / BORED	① ② ③ ④ ⑤ ⑥ ⑦ ⑧ ⑨ ⑩
SHORT ATTENTION	① ② ③ ④ ⑤ ⑥ ⑦ ⑧ ⑨ ⑩
FORGETFUL / CONFUSIONED	① ② ③ ④ ⑤ ⑥ ⑦ ⑧ ⑨ ⑩

HYPERACTIVITY

CONSTANTLY MOVING / TALKING	① ② ③ ④ ⑤ ⑥ ⑦ ⑧ ⑨ ⑩
STRUGGLING TO SIT STILL	① ② ③ ④ ⑤ ⑥ ⑦ ⑧ ⑨ ⑩
TOUCHING THINGS REPEATEDLY	① ② ③ ④ ⑤ ⑥ ⑦ ⑧ ⑨ ⑩
DIFFICULT SLEEPING	① ② ③ ④ ⑤ ⑥ ⑦ ⑧ ⑨ ⑩

IMPULSIVITY

ACTING WITHOUT THINKING	① ② ③ ④ ⑤ ⑥ ⑦ ⑧ ⑨ ⑩
INTERRUPTING OTHERS	① ② ③ ④ ⑤ ⑥ ⑦ ⑧ ⑨ ⑩
EASILY FRUSTRATED	① ② ③ ④ ⑤ ⑥ ⑦ ⑧ ⑨ ⑩
UNABLE TO HOLD BACK EMOTIONS	① ② ③ ④ ⑤ ⑥ ⑦ ⑧ ⑨ ⑩

MEALS

MEDICATIONS

Water Tracker

NOTES

....
....

<table>
<tr><td>

DAY GOALS

1 ....
2 ....
3 ....

</td><td>

DATE

WEEK

LOCATION

WEIGHT

</td></tr>
</table>

Mood Tracker 😟 😐 😖 😢 😠 😀

BEHAVIOR

INATTENTION

SHORT ATTENTION	① ② ③ ④ ⑤ ⑥ ⑦ ⑧ ⑨ ⑩
UNMOTIVATED / BORED	① ② ③ ④ ⑤ ⑥ ⑦ ⑧ ⑨ ⑩
SHORT ATTENTION	① ② ③ ④ ⑤ ⑥ ⑦ ⑧ ⑨ ⑩
FORGETFUL / CONFUSIONED	① ② ③ ④ ⑤ ⑥ ⑦ ⑧ ⑨ ⑩

HYPERACTIVITY

CONSTANTLY MOVING / TALKING	① ② ③ ④ ⑤ ⑥ ⑦ ⑧ ⑨ ⑩
STRUGGLING TO SIT STILL	① ② ③ ④ ⑤ ⑥ ⑦ ⑧ ⑨ ⑩
TOUCHING THINGS REPEATEDLY	① ② ③ ④ ⑤ ⑥ ⑦ ⑧ ⑨ ⑩
DIFFICULT SLEEPING	① ② ③ ④ ⑤ ⑥ ⑦ ⑧ ⑨ ⑩

IMPULSIVITY

ACTING WITHOUT THINKING	① ② ③ ④ ⑤ ⑥ ⑦ ⑧ ⑨ ⑩
INTERRUPTING OTHERS	① ② ③ ④ ⑤ ⑥ ⑦ ⑧ ⑨ ⑩
EASILY FRUSTRATED	① ② ③ ④ ⑤ ⑥ ⑦ ⑧ ⑨ ⑩
UNABLE TO HOLD BACK EMOTIONS	① ② ③ ④ ⑤ ⑥ ⑦ ⑧ ⑨ ⑩

MEALS

MEDICATIONS

Water Tracker 🍼 🍼 🍼 🍼 🍼 🍼 🍼 🍼

NOTES

....
....

<table>
<tr><td>

DAY GOALS

1 ....
2 ....
3 ....

</td><td>

DATE

WEEK

LOCATION

WEIGHT

</td></tr>
</table>

Mood Tracker

BEHAVIOR

INATTENTION

SHORT ATTENTION	① ② ③ ④ ⑤ ⑥ ⑦ ⑧ ⑨ ⑩
UNMOTIVATED / BORED	① ② ③ ④ ⑤ ⑥ ⑦ ⑧ ⑨ ⑩
SHORT ATTENTION	① ② ③ ④ ⑤ ⑥ ⑦ ⑧ ⑨ ⑩
FORGETFUL / CONFUSIONED	① ② ③ ④ ⑤ ⑥ ⑦ ⑧ ⑨ ⑩

HYPERACTIVITY

CONSTANTLY MOVING / TALKING	① ② ③ ④ ⑤ ⑥ ⑦ ⑧ ⑨ ⑩
STRUGGLING TO SIT STILL	① ② ③ ④ ⑤ ⑥ ⑦ ⑧ ⑨ ⑩
TOUCHING THINGS REPEATEDLY	① ② ③ ④ ⑤ ⑥ ⑦ ⑧ ⑨ ⑩
DIFFICULT SLEEPING	① ② ③ ④ ⑤ ⑥ ⑦ ⑧ ⑨ ⑩

IMPULSIVITY

ACTING WITHOUT THINKING	① ② ③ ④ ⑤ ⑥ ⑦ ⑧ ⑨ ⑩
INTERRUPTING OTHERS	① ② ③ ④ ⑤ ⑥ ⑦ ⑧ ⑨ ⑩
EASILY FRUSTRATED	① ② ③ ④ ⑤ ⑥ ⑦ ⑧ ⑨ ⑩
UNABLE TO HOLD BACK EMOTIONS	① ② ③ ④ ⑤ ⑥ ⑦ ⑧ ⑨ ⑩

MEALS	MEDICATIONS

Water Tracker

NOTES

....
....

<table>
<tr><td>

DAY GOALS

1 ....
2 ....
3 ....

</td><td>

DATE

WEEK

LOCATION

WEIGHT

</td></tr>
</table>

Mood Tracker

BEHAVIOR

INATTENTION

SHORT ATTENTION	① ② ③ ④ ⑤ ⑥ ⑦ ⑧ ⑨ ⑩
UNMOTIVATED / BORED	① ② ③ ④ ⑤ ⑥ ⑦ ⑧ ⑨ ⑩
SHORT ATTENTION	① ② ③ ④ ⑤ ⑥ ⑦ ⑧ ⑨ ⑩
FORGETFUL / CONFUSIONED	① ② ③ ④ ⑤ ⑥ ⑦ ⑧ ⑨ ⑩

HYPERACTIVITY

CONSTANTLY MOVING / TALKING	① ② ③ ④ ⑤ ⑥ ⑦ ⑧ ⑨ ⑩
STRUGGLING TO SIT STILL	① ② ③ ④ ⑤ ⑥ ⑦ ⑧ ⑨ ⑩
TOUCHING THINGS REPEATEDLY	① ② ③ ④ ⑤ ⑥ ⑦ ⑧ ⑨ ⑩
DIFFICULT SLEEPING	① ② ③ ④ ⑤ ⑥ ⑦ ⑧ ⑨ ⑩

IMPULSIVITY

ACTING WITHOUT THINKING	① ② ③ ④ ⑤ ⑥ ⑦ ⑧ ⑨ ⑩
INTERRUPTING OTHERS	① ② ③ ④ ⑤ ⑥ ⑦ ⑧ ⑨ ⑩
EASILY FRUSTRATED	① ② ③ ④ ⑤ ⑥ ⑦ ⑧ ⑨ ⑩
UNABLE TO HOLD BACK EMOTIONS	① ② ③ ④ ⑤ ⑥ ⑦ ⑧ ⑨ ⑩

MEALS	MEDICATIONS

Water Tracker

NOTES

....
....

1 ....
2 ....
3 ....

DATE

WEEK

LOCATION

WEIGHT

Mood Tracker

BEHAVIOR

INATTENTION

SHORT ATTENTION ① ② ③ ④ ⑤ ⑥ ⑦ ⑧ ⑨ ⑩

UNMOTIVATED / BORED ① ② ③ ④ ⑤ ⑥ ⑦ ⑧ ⑨ ⑩

SHORT ATTENTION ① ② ③ ④ ⑤ ⑥ ⑦ ⑧ ⑨ ⑩

FORGETFUL / CONFUSIONED ① ② ③ ④ ⑤ ⑥ ⑦ ⑧ ⑨ ⑩

HYPERACTIVITY

CONSTANTLY MOVING / TALKING ① ② ③ ④ ⑤ ⑥ ⑦ ⑧ ⑨ ⑩

STRUGGLING TO SIT STILL ① ② ③ ④ ⑤ ⑥ ⑦ ⑧ ⑨ ⑩

TOUCHING THINGS REPEATEDLY ① ② ③ ④ ⑤ ⑥ ⑦ ⑧ ⑨ ⑩

DIFFICULT SLEEPING ① ② ③ ④ ⑤ ⑥ ⑦ ⑧ ⑨ ⑩

IMPULSIVITY

ACTING WITHOUT THINKING ① ② ③ ④ ⑤ ⑥ ⑦ ⑧ ⑨ ⑩

INTERRUPTING OTHERS ① ② ③ ④ ⑤ ⑥ ⑦ ⑧ ⑨ ⑩

EASILY FRUSTRATED ① ② ③ ④ ⑤ ⑥ ⑦ ⑧ ⑨ ⑩

UNABLE TO HOLD BACK EMOTIONS ① ② ③ ④ ⑤ ⑥ ⑦ ⑧ ⑨ ⑩

MEALS

MEDICATIONS

Water Tracker

NOTES

....
....

<table>
<tr><td>

DAY GOALS

1 ....
2 ....
3 ....

</td><td>

DATE

WEEK

LOCATION

WEIGHT

</td></tr>
</table>

Mood Tracker

BEHAVIOR

INATTENTION

SHORT ATTENTION	① ② ③ ④ ⑤ ⑥ ⑦ ⑧ ⑨ ⑩
UNMOTIVATED / BORED	① ② ③ ④ ⑤ ⑥ ⑦ ⑧ ⑨ ⑩
SHORT ATTENTION	① ② ③ ④ ⑤ ⑥ ⑦ ⑧ ⑨ ⑩
FORGETFUL / CONFUSIONED	① ② ③ ④ ⑤ ⑥ ⑦ ⑧ ⑨ ⑩

HYPERACTIVITY

CONSTANTLY MOVING / TALKING	① ② ③ ④ ⑤ ⑥ ⑦ ⑧ ⑨ ⑩
STRUGGLING TO SIT STILL	① ② ③ ④ ⑤ ⑥ ⑦ ⑧ ⑨ ⑩
TOUCHING THINGS REPEATEDLY	① ② ③ ④ ⑤ ⑥ ⑦ ⑧ ⑨ ⑩
DIFFICULT SLEEPING	① ② ③ ④ ⑤ ⑥ ⑦ ⑧ ⑨ ⑩

IMPULSIVITY

ACTING WITHOUT THINKING	① ② ③ ④ ⑤ ⑥ ⑦ ⑧ ⑨ ⑩
INTERRUPTING OTHERS	① ② ③ ④ ⑤ ⑥ ⑦ ⑧ ⑨ ⑩
EASILY FRUSTRATED	① ② ③ ④ ⑤ ⑥ ⑦ ⑧ ⑨ ⑩
UNABLE TO HOLD BACK EMOTIONS	① ② ③ ④ ⑤ ⑥ ⑦ ⑧ ⑨ ⑩

MEALS	MEDICATIONS

Water Tracker

NOTES

....
....

DAY GOALS

1 ....
2 ....
3 ....

DATE

WEEK

LOCATION

WEIGHT

Mood Tracker

BEHAVIOR

INATTENTION

SHORT ATTENTION	① ② ③ ④ ⑤ ⑥ ⑦ ⑧ ⑨ ⑩
UNMOTIVATED / BORED	① ② ③ ④ ⑤ ⑥ ⑦ ⑧ ⑨ ⑩
SHORT ATTENTION	① ② ③ ④ ⑤ ⑥ ⑦ ⑧ ⑨ ⑩
FORGETFUL / CONFUSIONED	① ② ③ ④ ⑤ ⑥ ⑦ ⑧ ⑨ ⑩

HYPERACTIVITY

CONSTANTLY MOVING / TALKING	① ② ③ ④ ⑤ ⑥ ⑦ ⑧ ⑨ ⑩
STRUGGLING TO SIT STILL	① ② ③ ④ ⑤ ⑥ ⑦ ⑧ ⑨ ⑩
TOUCHING THINGS REPEATEDLY	① ② ③ ④ ⑤ ⑥ ⑦ ⑧ ⑨ ⑩
DIFFICULT SLEEPING	① ② ③ ④ ⑤ ⑥ ⑦ ⑧ ⑨ ⑩

IMPULSIVITY

ACTING WITHOUT THINKING	① ② ③ ④ ⑤ ⑥ ⑦ ⑧ ⑨ ⑩
INTERRUPTING OTHERS	① ② ③ ④ ⑤ ⑥ ⑦ ⑧ ⑨ ⑩
EASILY FRUSTRATED	① ② ③ ④ ⑤ ⑥ ⑦ ⑧ ⑨ ⑩
UNABLE TO HOLD BACK EMOTIONS	① ② ③ ④ ⑤ ⑥ ⑦ ⑧ ⑨ ⑩

MEALS

MEDICATIONS

Water Tracker

NOTES

....
....

<table>
<tr><td>

DAY GOALS

1 ....
2 ....
3 ....

</td><td>

DATE
WEEK
LOCATION
WEIGHT

</td></tr>
</table>

Mood Tracker

BEHAVIOR

INATTENTION

SHORT ATTENTION	① ② ③ ④ ⑤ ⑥ ⑦ ⑧ ⑨ ⑩
UNMOTIVATED / BORED	① ② ③ ④ ⑤ ⑥ ⑦ ⑧ ⑨ ⑩
SHORT ATTENTION	① ② ③ ④ ⑤ ⑥ ⑦ ⑧ ⑨ ⑩
FORGETFUL / CONFUSIONED	① ② ③ ④ ⑤ ⑥ ⑦ ⑧ ⑨ ⑩

HYPERACTIVITY

CONSTANTLY MOVING / TALKING	① ② ③ ④ ⑤ ⑥ ⑦ ⑧ ⑨ ⑩
STRUGGLING TO SIT STILL	① ② ③ ④ ⑤ ⑥ ⑦ ⑧ ⑨ ⑩
TOUCHING THINGS REPEATEDLY	① ② ③ ④ ⑤ ⑥ ⑦ ⑧ ⑨ ⑩
DIFFICULT SLEEPING	① ② ③ ④ ⑤ ⑥ ⑦ ⑧ ⑨ ⑩

IMPULSIVITY

ACTING WITHOUT THINKING	① ② ③ ④ ⑤ ⑥ ⑦ ⑧ ⑨ ⑩
INTERRUPTING OTHERS	① ② ③ ④ ⑤ ⑥ ⑦ ⑧ ⑨ ⑩
EASILY FRUSTRATED	① ② ③ ④ ⑤ ⑥ ⑦ ⑧ ⑨ ⑩
UNABLE TO HOLD BACK EMOTIONS	① ② ③ ④ ⑤ ⑥ ⑦ ⑧ ⑨ ⑩

MEALS	MEDICATIONS

Water Tracker

NOTES

....
....

<table><tr><td>

DAY GOALS

1 ....
2 ....
3 ....

</td><td>

DATE

WEEK

LOCATION

WEIGHT

</td></tr></table>

Mood Tracker

BEHAVIOR

INATTENTION

SHORT ATTENTION	① ② ③ ④ ⑤ ⑥ ⑦ ⑧ ⑨ ⑩
UNMOTIVATED / BORED	① ② ③ ④ ⑤ ⑥ ⑦ ⑧ ⑨ ⑩
SHORT ATTENTION	① ② ③ ④ ⑤ ⑥ ⑦ ⑧ ⑨ ⑩
FORGETFUL / CONFUSIONED	① ② ③ ④ ⑤ ⑥ ⑦ ⑧ ⑨ ⑩

HYPERACTIVITY

CONSTANTLY MOVING / TALKING	① ② ③ ④ ⑤ ⑥ ⑦ ⑧ ⑨ ⑩
STRUGGLING TO SIT STILL	① ② ③ ④ ⑤ ⑥ ⑦ ⑧ ⑨ ⑩
TOUCHING THINGS REPEATEDLY	① ② ③ ④ ⑤ ⑥ ⑦ ⑧ ⑨ ⑩
DIFFICULT SLEEPING	① ② ③ ④ ⑤ ⑥ ⑦ ⑧ ⑨ ⑩

IMPULSIVITY

ACTING WITHOUT THINKING	① ② ③ ④ ⑤ ⑥ ⑦ ⑧ ⑨ ⑩
INTERRUPTING OTHERS	① ② ③ ④ ⑤ ⑥ ⑦ ⑧ ⑨ ⑩
EASILY FRUSTRATED	① ② ③ ④ ⑤ ⑥ ⑦ ⑧ ⑨ ⑩
UNABLE TO HOLD BACK EMOTIONS	① ② ③ ④ ⑤ ⑥ ⑦ ⑧ ⑨ ⑩

MEALS	MEDICATIONS

Water Tracker

NOTES

....
....

<table><tr><td>

DAY GOALS

1 ....
2 ....
3 ....

</td><td>

DATE

WEEK

LOCATION

WEIGHT

</td></tr></table>

Mood Tracker

BEHAVIOR

INATTENTION

SHORT ATTENTION   ① ② ③ ④ ⑤ ⑥ ⑦ ⑧ ⑨ ⑩

UNMOTIVATED / BORED   ① ② ③ ④ ⑤ ⑥ ⑦ ⑧ ⑨ ⑩

SHORT ATTENTION   ① ② ③ ④ ⑤ ⑥ ⑦ ⑧ ⑨ ⑩

FORGETFUL / CONFUSIONED   ① ② ③ ④ ⑤ ⑥ ⑦ ⑧ ⑨ ⑩

HYPERACTIVITY

CONSTANTLY MOVING / TALKING   ① ② ③ ④ ⑤ ⑥ ⑦ ⑧ ⑨ ⑩

STRUGGLING TO SIT STILL   ① ② ③ ④ ⑤ ⑥ ⑦ ⑧ ⑨ ⑩

TOUCHING THINGS REPEATEDLY   ① ② ③ ④ ⑤ ⑥ ⑦ ⑧ ⑨ ⑩

DIFFICULT SLEEPING   ① ② ③ ④ ⑤ ⑥ ⑦ ⑧ ⑨ ⑩

IMPULSIVITY

ACTING WITHOUT THINKING   ① ② ③ ④ ⑤ ⑥ ⑦ ⑧ ⑨ ⑩

INTERRUPTING OTHERS   ① ② ③ ④ ⑤ ⑥ ⑦ ⑧ ⑨ ⑩

EASILY FRUSTRATED   ① ② ③ ④ ⑤ ⑥ ⑦ ⑧ ⑨ ⑩

UNABLE TO HOLD BACK EMOTIONS   ① ② ③ ④ ⑤ ⑥ ⑦ ⑧ ⑨ ⑩

MEALS

MEDICATIONS

Water Tracker

NOTES

....
....

Mood Tracker

BEHAVIOR

INATTENTION

SHORT ATTENTION	① ② ③ ④ ⑤ ⑥ ⑦ ⑧ ⑨ ⑩
UNMOTIVATED / BORED	① ② ③ ④ ⑤ ⑥ ⑦ ⑧ ⑨ ⑩
SHORT ATTENTION	① ② ③ ④ ⑤ ⑥ ⑦ ⑧ ⑨ ⑩
FORGETFUL / CONFUSIONED	① ② ③ ④ ⑤ ⑥ ⑦ ⑧ ⑨ ⑩

HYPERACTIVITY

CONSTANTLY MOVING / TALKING	① ② ③ ④ ⑤ ⑥ ⑦ ⑧ ⑨ ⑩
STRUGGLING TO SIT STILL	① ② ③ ④ ⑤ ⑥ ⑦ ⑧ ⑨ ⑩
TOUCHING THINGS REPEATEDLY	① ② ③ ④ ⑤ ⑥ ⑦ ⑧ ⑨ ⑩
DIFFICULT SLEEPING	① ② ③ ④ ⑤ ⑥ ⑦ ⑧ ⑨ ⑩

IMPULSIVITY

ACTING WITHOUT THINKING	① ② ③ ④ ⑤ ⑥ ⑦ ⑧ ⑨ ⑩
INTERRUPTING OTHERS	① ② ③ ④ ⑤ ⑥ ⑦ ⑧ ⑨ ⑩
EASILY FRUSTRATED	① ② ③ ④ ⑤ ⑥ ⑦ ⑧ ⑨ ⑩
UNABLE TO HOLD BACK EMOTIONS	① ② ③ ④ ⑤ ⑥ ⑦ ⑧ ⑨ ⑩

MEALS

MEDICATIONS

Water Tracker

NOTES

1 ....
2 ....
3 ....

DATE
WEEK
LOCATION
WEIGHT

Mood Tracker

BEHAVIOR

INATTENTION

SHORT ATTENTION	1 2 3 4 5 6 7 8 9 10
UNMOTIVATED / BORED	1 2 3 4 5 6 7 8 9 10
SHORT ATTENTION	1 2 3 4 5 6 7 8 9 10
FORGETFUL / CONFUSIONED	1 2 3 4 5 6 7 8 9 10

HYPERACTIVITY

CONSTANTLY MOVING / TALKING	1 2 3 4 5 6 7 8 9 10
STRUGGLING TO SIT STILL	1 2 3 4 5 6 7 8 9 10
TOUCHING THINGS REPEATEDLY	1 2 3 4 5 6 7 8 9 10
DIFFICULT SLEEPING	1 2 3 4 5 6 7 8 9 10

IMPULSIVITY

ACTING WITHOUT THINKING	1 2 3 4 5 6 7 8 9 10
INTERRUPTING OTHERS	1 2 3 4 5 6 7 8 9 10
EASILY FRUSTRATED	1 2 3 4 5 6 7 8 9 10
UNABLE TO HOLD BACK EMOTIONS	1 2 3 4 5 6 7 8 9 10

MEALS

MEDICATIONS

Water Tracker

NOTES

....
....

1 ....
2 ....
3 ....

DATE

WEEK

LOCATION

WEIGHT

Mood Tracker

BEHAVIOR

INATTENTION

SHORT ATTENTION	① ② ③ ④ ⑤ ⑥ ⑦ ⑧ ⑨ ⑩
UNMOTIVATED / BORED	① ② ③ ④ ⑤ ⑥ ⑦ ⑧ ⑨ ⑩
SHORT ATTENTION	① ② ③ ④ ⑤ ⑥ ⑦ ⑧ ⑨ ⑩
FORGETFUL / CONFUSIONED	① ② ③ ④ ⑤ ⑥ ⑦ ⑧ ⑨ ⑩

HYPERACTIVITY

CONSTANTLY MOVING / TALKING	① ② ③ ④ ⑤ ⑥ ⑦ ⑧ ⑨ ⑩
STRUGGLING TO SIT STILL	① ② ③ ④ ⑤ ⑥ ⑦ ⑧ ⑨ ⑩
TOUCHING THINGS REPEATEDLY	① ② ③ ④ ⑤ ⑥ ⑦ ⑧ ⑨ ⑩
DIFFICULT SLEEPING	① ② ③ ④ ⑤ ⑥ ⑦ ⑧ ⑨ ⑩

IMPULSIVITY

ACTING WITHOUT THINKING	① ② ③ ④ ⑤ ⑥ ⑦ ⑧ ⑨ ⑩
INTERRUPTING OTHERS	① ② ③ ④ ⑤ ⑥ ⑦ ⑧ ⑨ ⑩
EASILY FRUSTRATED	① ② ③ ④ ⑤ ⑥ ⑦ ⑧ ⑨ ⑩
UNABLE TO HOLD BACK EMOTIONS	① ② ③ ④ ⑤ ⑥ ⑦ ⑧ ⑨ ⑩

MEALS

MEDICATIONS

Water Tracker

NOTES

....
....

<table>
<tr><td>

DAY GOALS

1 ....
2 ....
3 ....

</td><td>

DATE

WEEK

LOCATION

WEIGHT

</td></tr>
</table>

Mood Tracker

BEHAVIOR

INATTENTION

SHORT ATTENTION	① ② ③ ④ ⑤ ⑥ ⑦ ⑧ ⑨ ⑩
UNMOTIVATED / BORED	① ② ③ ④ ⑤ ⑥ ⑦ ⑧ ⑨ ⑩
SHORT ATTENTION	① ② ③ ④ ⑤ ⑥ ⑦ ⑧ ⑨ ⑩
FORGETFUL / CONFUSIONED	① ② ③ ④ ⑤ ⑥ ⑦ ⑧ ⑨ ⑩

HYPERACTIVITY

CONSTANTLY MOVING / TALKING	① ② ③ ④ ⑤ ⑥ ⑦ ⑧ ⑨ ⑩
STRUGGLING TO SIT STILL	① ② ③ ④ ⑤ ⑥ ⑦ ⑧ ⑨ ⑩
TOUCHING THINGS REPEATEDLY	① ② ③ ④ ⑤ ⑥ ⑦ ⑧ ⑨ ⑩
DIFFICULT SLEEPING	① ② ③ ④ ⑤ ⑥ ⑦ ⑧ ⑨ ⑩

IMPULSIVITY

ACTING WITHOUT THINKING	① ② ③ ④ ⑤ ⑥ ⑦ ⑧ ⑨ ⑩
INTERRUPTING OTHERS	① ② ③ ④ ⑤ ⑥ ⑦ ⑧ ⑨ ⑩
EASILY FRUSTRATED	① ② ③ ④ ⑤ ⑥ ⑦ ⑧ ⑨ ⑩
UNABLE TO HOLD BACK EMOTIONS	① ② ③ ④ ⑤ ⑥ ⑦ ⑧ ⑨ ⑩

MEALS

MEDICATIONS

Water Tracker

NOTES

....
....

Mood Tracker

BEHAVIOR

INATTENTION

SHORT ATTENTION — ① ② ③ ④ ⑤ ⑥ ⑦ ⑧ ⑨ ⑩
UNMOTIVATED / BORED — ① ② ③ ④ ⑤ ⑥ ⑦ ⑧ ⑨ ⑩
SHORT ATTENTION — ① ② ③ ④ ⑤ ⑥ ⑦ ⑧ ⑨ ⑩
FORGETFUL / CONFUSIONED — ① ② ③ ④ ⑤ ⑥ ⑦ ⑧ ⑨ ⑩

HYPERACTIVITY

CONSTANTLY MOVING / TALKING — ① ② ③ ④ ⑤ ⑥ ⑦ ⑧ ⑨ ⑩
STRUGGLING TO SIT STILL — ① ② ③ ④ ⑤ ⑥ ⑦ ⑧ ⑨ ⑩
TOUCHING THINGS REPEATEDLY — ① ② ③ ④ ⑤ ⑥ ⑦ ⑧ ⑨ ⑩
DIFFICULT SLEEPING — ① ② ③ ④ ⑤ ⑥ ⑦ ⑧ ⑨ ⑩

IMPULSIVITY

ACTING WITHOUT THINKING — ① ② ③ ④ ⑤ ⑥ ⑦ ⑧ ⑨ ⑩
INTERRUPTING OTHERS — ① ② ③ ④ ⑤ ⑥ ⑦ ⑧ ⑨ ⑩
EASILY FRUSTRATED — ① ② ③ ④ ⑤ ⑥ ⑦ ⑧ ⑨ ⑩
UNABLE TO HOLD BACK EMOTIONS — ① ② ③ ④ ⑤ ⑥ ⑦ ⑧ ⑨ ⑩

MEALS

MEDICATIONS

Water Tracker

NOTES

....
....

DAY GOALS

1 ....
2 ....
3 ....

DATE

WEEK

LOCATION

WEIGHT

Mood Tracker ☹ 😐 😖 😢 😠 😀

BEHAVIOR

INATTENTION

SHORT ATTENTION	① ② ③ ④ ⑤ ⑥ ⑦ ⑧ ⑨ ⑩
UNMOTIVATED / BORED	① ② ③ ④ ⑤ ⑥ ⑦ ⑧ ⑨ ⑩
SHORT ATTENTION	① ② ③ ④ ⑤ ⑥ ⑦ ⑧ ⑨ ⑩
FORGETFUL / CONFUSIONED	① ② ③ ④ ⑤ ⑥ ⑦ ⑧ ⑨ ⑩

HYPERACTIVITY

CONSTANTLY MOVING / TALKING	① ② ③ ④ ⑤ ⑥ ⑦ ⑧ ⑨ ⑩
STRUGGLING TO SIT STILL	① ② ③ ④ ⑤ ⑥ ⑦ ⑧ ⑨ ⑩
TOUCHING THINGS REPEATEDLY	① ② ③ ④ ⑤ ⑥ ⑦ ⑧ ⑨ ⑩
DIFFICULT SLEEPING	① ② ③ ④ ⑤ ⑥ ⑦ ⑧ ⑨ ⑩

IMPULSIVITY

ACTING WITHOUT THINKING	① ② ③ ④ ⑤ ⑥ ⑦ ⑧ ⑨ ⑩
INTERRUPTING OTHERS	① ② ③ ④ ⑤ ⑥ ⑦ ⑧ ⑨ ⑩
EASILY FRUSTRATED	① ② ③ ④ ⑤ ⑥ ⑦ ⑧ ⑨ ⑩
UNABLE TO HOLD BACK EMOTIONS	① ② ③ ④ ⑤ ⑥ ⑦ ⑧ ⑨ ⑩

MEALS

MEDICATIONS

Water Tracker 🍼 🍼 🍼 🍼 🍼 🍼 🍼 🍼

NOTES

....
....

DAY GOALS

1 ....
2 ....
3 ....

DATE
WEEK
LOCATION
WEIGHT

Mood Tracker

BEHAVIOR

INATTENTION

SHORT ATTENTION	① ② ③ ④ ⑤ ⑥ ⑦ ⑧ ⑨ ⑩
UNMOTIVATED / BORED	① ② ③ ④ ⑤ ⑥ ⑦ ⑧ ⑨ ⑩
SHORT ATTENTION	① ② ③ ④ ⑤ ⑥ ⑦ ⑧ ⑨ ⑩
FORGETFUL / CONFUSIONED	① ② ③ ④ ⑤ ⑥ ⑦ ⑧ ⑨ ⑩

HYPERACTIVITY

CONSTANTLY MOVING / TALKING	① ② ③ ④ ⑤ ⑥ ⑦ ⑧ ⑨ ⑩
STRUGGLING TO SIT STILL	① ② ③ ④ ⑤ ⑥ ⑦ ⑧ ⑨ ⑩
TOUCHING THINGS REPEATEDLY	① ② ③ ④ ⑤ ⑥ ⑦ ⑧ ⑨ ⑩
DIFFICULT SLEEPING	① ② ③ ④ ⑤ ⑥ ⑦ ⑧ ⑨ ⑩

IMPULSIVITY

ACTING WITHOUT THINKING	① ② ③ ④ ⑤ ⑥ ⑦ ⑧ ⑨ ⑩
INTERRUPTING OTHERS	① ② ③ ④ ⑤ ⑥ ⑦ ⑧ ⑨ ⑩
EASILY FRUSTRATED	① ② ③ ④ ⑤ ⑥ ⑦ ⑧ ⑨ ⑩
UNABLE TO HOLD BACK EMOTIONS	① ② ③ ④ ⑤ ⑥ ⑦ ⑧ ⑨ ⑩

MEALS

MEDICATIONS

Water Tracker

NOTES

....
....

DATE

WEEK

LOCATION

WEIGHT

Mood Tracker

BEHAVIOR

INATTENTION

SHORT ATTENTION	① ② ③ ④ ⑤ ⑥ ⑦ ⑧ ⑨ ⑩
UNMOTIVATED / BORED	① ② ③ ④ ⑤ ⑥ ⑦ ⑧ ⑨ ⑩
SHORT ATTENTION	① ② ③ ④ ⑤ ⑥ ⑦ ⑧ ⑨ ⑩
FORGETFUL / CONFUSIONED	① ② ③ ④ ⑤ ⑥ ⑦ ⑧ ⑨ ⑩

HYPERACTIVITY

CONSTANTLY MOVING / TALKING	① ② ③ ④ ⑤ ⑥ ⑦ ⑧ ⑨ ⑩
STRUGGLING TO SIT STILL	① ② ③ ④ ⑤ ⑥ ⑦ ⑧ ⑨ ⑩
TOUCHING THINGS REPEATEDLY	① ② ③ ④ ⑤ ⑥ ⑦ ⑧ ⑨ ⑩
DIFFICULT SLEEPING	① ② ③ ④ ⑤ ⑥ ⑦ ⑧ ⑨ ⑩

IMPULSIVITY

ACTING WITHOUT THINKING	① ② ③ ④ ⑤ ⑥ ⑦ ⑧ ⑨ ⑩
INTERRUPTING OTHERS	① ② ③ ④ ⑤ ⑥ ⑦ ⑧ ⑨ ⑩
EASILY FRUSTRATED	① ② ③ ④ ⑤ ⑥ ⑦ ⑧ ⑨ ⑩
UNABLE TO HOLD BACK EMOTIONS	① ② ③ ④ ⑤ ⑥ ⑦ ⑧ ⑨ ⑩

MEALS

MEDICATIONS

Water Tracker

NOTES

<table>
<tr><td>

DAY GOALS

1 ....
2 ....
3 ....

</td><td>

DATE

WEEK

LOCATION

WEIGHT

</td></tr>
</table>

Mood Tracker

BEHAVIOR

INATTENTION

SHORT ATTENTION	① ② ③ ④ ⑤ ⑥ ⑦ ⑧ ⑨ ⑩
UNMOTIVATED / BORED	① ② ③ ④ ⑤ ⑥ ⑦ ⑧ ⑨ ⑩
SHORT ATTENTION	① ② ③ ④ ⑤ ⑥ ⑦ ⑧ ⑨ ⑩
FORGETFUL / CONFUSIONED	① ② ③ ④ ⑤ ⑥ ⑦ ⑧ ⑨ ⑩

HYPERACTIVITY

CONSTANTLY MOVING / TALKING	① ② ③ ④ ⑤ ⑥ ⑦ ⑧ ⑨ ⑩
STRUGGLING TO SIT STILL	① ② ③ ④ ⑤ ⑥ ⑦ ⑧ ⑨ ⑩
TOUCHING THINGS REPEATEDLY	① ② ③ ④ ⑤ ⑥ ⑦ ⑧ ⑨ ⑩
DIFFICULT SLEEPING	① ② ③ ④ ⑤ ⑥ ⑦ ⑧ ⑨ ⑩

IMPULSIVITY

ACTING WITHOUT THINKING	① ② ③ ④ ⑤ ⑥ ⑦ ⑧ ⑨ ⑩
INTERRUPTING OTHERS	① ② ③ ④ ⑤ ⑥ ⑦ ⑧ ⑨ ⑩
EASILY FRUSTRATED	① ② ③ ④ ⑤ ⑥ ⑦ ⑧ ⑨ ⑩
UNABLE TO HOLD BACK EMOTIONS	① ② ③ ④ ⑤ ⑥ ⑦ ⑧ ⑨ ⑩

MEALS

MEDICATIONS

Water Tracker

NOTES

....
....

DAY GOALS

1 ....
2 ....
3 ....

DATE
WEEK
LOCATION
WEIGHT

Mood Tracker

BEHAVIOR

INATTENTION

SHORT ATTENTION	1 2 3 4 5 6 7 8 9 10
UNMOTIVATED / BORED	1 2 3 4 5 6 7 8 9 10
SHORT ATTENTION	1 2 3 4 5 6 7 8 9 10
FORGETFUL / CONFUSIONED	1 2 3 4 5 6 7 8 9 10

HYPERACTIVITY

CONSTANTLY MOVING / TALKING	1 2 3 4 5 6 7 8 9 10
STRUGGLING TO SIT STILL	1 2 3 4 5 6 7 8 9 10
TOUCHING THINGS REPEATEDLY	1 2 3 4 5 6 7 8 9 10
DIFFICULT SLEEPING	1 2 3 4 5 6 7 8 9 10

IMPULSIVITY

ACTING WITHOUT THINKING	1 2 3 4 5 6 7 8 9 10
INTERRUPTING OTHERS	1 2 3 4 5 6 7 8 9 10
EASILY FRUSTRATED	1 2 3 4 5 6 7 8 9 10
UNABLE TO HOLD BACK EMOTIONS	1 2 3 4 5 6 7 8 9 10

MEALS

MEDICATIONS

Water Tracker

NOTES

....
....

<table>
<tr><td>

DAY GOALS

1 ....
2 ....
3 ....

</td><td>

DATE

WEEK

LOCATION

WEIGHT

</td></tr>
</table>

Mood Tracker

BEHAVIOR

INATTENTION

SHORT ATTENTION	① ② ③ ④ ⑤ ⑥ ⑦ ⑧ ⑨ ⑩
UNMOTIVATED / BORED	① ② ③ ④ ⑤ ⑥ ⑦ ⑧ ⑨ ⑩
SHORT ATTENTION	① ② ③ ④ ⑤ ⑥ ⑦ ⑧ ⑨ ⑩
FORGETFUL / CONFUSIONED	① ② ③ ④ ⑤ ⑥ ⑦ ⑧ ⑨ ⑩

HYPERACTIVITY

CONSTANTLY MOVING / TALKING	① ② ③ ④ ⑤ ⑥ ⑦ ⑧ ⑨ ⑩
STRUGGLING TO SIT STILL	① ② ③ ④ ⑤ ⑥ ⑦ ⑧ ⑨ ⑩
TOUCHING THINGS REPEATEDLY	① ② ③ ④ ⑤ ⑥ ⑦ ⑧ ⑨ ⑩
DIFFICULT SLEEPING	① ② ③ ④ ⑤ ⑥ ⑦ ⑧ ⑨ ⑩

IMPULSIVITY

ACTING WITHOUT THINKING	① ② ③ ④ ⑤ ⑥ ⑦ ⑧ ⑨ ⑩
INTERRUPTING OTHERS	① ② ③ ④ ⑤ ⑥ ⑦ ⑧ ⑨ ⑩
EASILY FRUSTRATED	① ② ③ ④ ⑤ ⑥ ⑦ ⑧ ⑨ ⑩
UNABLE TO HOLD BACK EMOTIONS	① ② ③ ④ ⑤ ⑥ ⑦ ⑧ ⑨ ⑩

MEALS

MEDICATIONS

Water Tracker

NOTES

....
....

Mood Tracker

BEHAVIOR

INATTENTION

SHORT ATTENTION	1 2 3 4 5 6 7 8 9 10
UNMOTIVATED / BORED	1 2 3 4 5 6 7 8 9 10
SHORT ATTENTION	1 2 3 4 5 6 7 8 9 10
FORGETFUL / CONFUSIONED	1 2 3 4 5 6 7 8 9 10

HYPERACTIVITY

CONSTANTLY MOVING / TALKING	1 2 3 4 5 6 7 8 9 10
STRUGGLING TO SIT STILL	1 2 3 4 5 6 7 8 9 10
TOUCHING THINGS REPEATEDLY	1 2 3 4 5 6 7 8 9 10
DIFFICULT SLEEPING	1 2 3 4 5 6 7 8 9 10

IMPULSIVITY

ACTING WITHOUT THINKING	1 2 3 4 5 6 7 8 9 10
INTERRUPTING OTHERS	1 2 3 4 5 6 7 8 9 10
EASILY FRUSTRATED	1 2 3 4 5 6 7 8 9 10
UNABLE TO HOLD BACK EMOTIONS	1 2 3 4 5 6 7 8 9 10

MEALS

MEDICATIONS

Water Tracker

NOTES

<table>
<tr><td>

DAY GOALS

1 ....
2 ....
3 ....

</td><td>

DATE

WEEK

LOCATION

WEIGHT

</td></tr>
</table>

Mood Tracker ☹ 😐 😖 😢 😠 😃

BEHAVIOR

INATTENTION

SHORT ATTENTION	① ② ③ ④ ⑤ ⑥ ⑦ ⑧ ⑨ ⑩
UNMOTIVATED / BORED	① ② ③ ④ ⑤ ⑥ ⑦ ⑧ ⑨ ⑩
SHORT ATTENTION	① ② ③ ④ ⑤ ⑥ ⑦ ⑧ ⑨ ⑩
FORGETFUL / CONFUSIONED	① ② ③ ④ ⑤ ⑥ ⑦ ⑧ ⑨ ⑩

HYPERACTIVITY

CONSTANTLY MOVING / TALKING	① ② ③ ④ ⑤ ⑥ ⑦ ⑧ ⑨ ⑩
STRUGGLING TO SIT STILL	① ② ③ ④ ⑤ ⑥ ⑦ ⑧ ⑨ ⑩
TOUCHING THINGS REPEATEDLY	① ② ③ ④ ⑤ ⑥ ⑦ ⑧ ⑨ ⑩
DIFFICULT SLEEPING	① ② ③ ④ ⑤ ⑥ ⑦ ⑧ ⑨ ⑩

IMPULSIVITY

ACTING WITHOUT THINKING	① ② ③ ④ ⑤ ⑥ ⑦ ⑧ ⑨ ⑩
INTERRUPTING OTHERS	① ② ③ ④ ⑤ ⑥ ⑦ ⑧ ⑨ ⑩
EASILY FRUSTRATED	① ② ③ ④ ⑤ ⑥ ⑦ ⑧ ⑨ ⑩
UNABLE TO HOLD BACK EMOTIONS	① ② ③ ④ ⑤ ⑥ ⑦ ⑧ ⑨ ⑩

MEALS	MEDICATIONS

Water Tracker 🍼 🍼 🍼 🍼 🍼 🍼 🍼 🍼

NOTES

....
....

DATE

WEEK

LOCATION

WEIGHT

Mood Tracker

BEHAVIOR

INATTENTION

SHORT ATTENTION	① ② ③ ④ ⑤ ⑥ ⑦ ⑧ ⑨ ⑩
UNMOTIVATED / BORED	① ② ③ ④ ⑤ ⑥ ⑦ ⑧ ⑨ ⑩
SHORT ATTENTION	① ② ③ ④ ⑤ ⑥ ⑦ ⑧ ⑨ ⑩
FORGETFUL / CONFUSIONED	① ② ③ ④ ⑤ ⑥ ⑦ ⑧ ⑨ ⑩

HYPERACTIVITY

CONSTANTLY MOVING / TALKING	① ② ③ ④ ⑤ ⑥ ⑦ ⑧ ⑨ ⑩
STRUGGLING TO SIT STILL	① ② ③ ④ ⑤ ⑥ ⑦ ⑧ ⑨ ⑩
TOUCHING THINGS REPEATEDLY	① ② ③ ④ ⑤ ⑥ ⑦ ⑧ ⑨ ⑩
DIFFICULT SLEEPING	① ② ③ ④ ⑤ ⑥ ⑦ ⑧ ⑨ ⑩

IMPULSIVITY

ACTING WITHOUT THINKING	① ② ③ ④ ⑤ ⑥ ⑦ ⑧ ⑨ ⑩
INTERRUPTING OTHERS	① ② ③ ④ ⑤ ⑥ ⑦ ⑧ ⑨ ⑩
EASILY FRUSTRATED	① ② ③ ④ ⑤ ⑥ ⑦ ⑧ ⑨ ⑩
UNABLE TO HOLD BACK EMOTIONS	① ② ③ ④ ⑤ ⑥ ⑦ ⑧ ⑨ ⑩

MEALS

MEDICATIONS

Water Tracker

NOTES

....
....

Mood Tracker

BEHAVIOR

INATTENTION

SHORT ATTENTION ① ② ③ ④ ⑤ ⑥ ⑦ ⑧ ⑨ ⑩
UNMOTIVATED / BORED ① ② ③ ④ ⑤ ⑥ ⑦ ⑧ ⑨ ⑩
SHORT ATTENTION ① ② ③ ④ ⑤ ⑥ ⑦ ⑧ ⑨ ⑩
FORGETFUL / CONFUSIONED ① ② ③ ④ ⑤ ⑥ ⑦ ⑧ ⑨ ⑩

HYPERACTIVITY

CONSTANTLY MOVING / TALKING ① ② ③ ④ ⑤ ⑥ ⑦ ⑧ ⑨ ⑩
STRUGGLING TO SIT STILL ① ② ③ ④ ⑤ ⑥ ⑦ ⑧ ⑨ ⑩
TOUCHING THINGS REPEATEDLY ① ② ③ ④ ⑤ ⑥ ⑦ ⑧ ⑨ ⑩
DIFFICULT SLEEPING ① ② ③ ④ ⑤ ⑥ ⑦ ⑧ ⑨ ⑩

IMPULSIVITY

ACTING WITHOUT THINKING ① ② ③ ④ ⑤ ⑥ ⑦ ⑧ ⑨ ⑩
INTERRUPTING OTHERS ① ② ③ ④ ⑤ ⑥ ⑦ ⑧ ⑨ ⑩
EASILY FRUSTRATED ① ② ③ ④ ⑤ ⑥ ⑦ ⑧ ⑨ ⑩
UNABLE TO HOLD BACK EMOTIONS ① ② ③ ④ ⑤ ⑥ ⑦ ⑧ ⑨ ⑩

MEALS

MEDICATIONS

Water Tracker

NOTES

....
....

<table>
<tr><td>

DAY GOALS

1 ....
2 ....
3 ....

</td><td>

DATE

WEEK

LOCATION

WEIGHT

</td></tr>
</table>

Mood Tracker

BEHAVIOR

INATTENTION

SHORT ATTENTION	① ② ③ ④ ⑤ ⑥ ⑦ ⑧ ⑨ ⑩
UNMOTIVATED / BORED	① ② ③ ④ ⑤ ⑥ ⑦ ⑧ ⑨ ⑩
SHORT ATTENTION	① ② ③ ④ ⑤ ⑥ ⑦ ⑧ ⑨ ⑩
FORGETFUL / CONFUSIONED	① ② ③ ④ ⑤ ⑥ ⑦ ⑧ ⑨ ⑩

HYPERACTIVITY

CONSTANTLY MOVING / TALKING	① ② ③ ④ ⑤ ⑥ ⑦ ⑧ ⑨ ⑩
STRUGGLING TO SIT STILL	① ② ③ ④ ⑤ ⑥ ⑦ ⑧ ⑨ ⑩
TOUCHING THINGS REPEATEDLY	① ② ③ ④ ⑤ ⑥ ⑦ ⑧ ⑨ ⑩
DIFFICULT SLEEPING	① ② ③ ④ ⑤ ⑥ ⑦ ⑧ ⑨ ⑩

IMPULSIVITY

ACTING WITHOUT THINKING	① ② ③ ④ ⑤ ⑥ ⑦ ⑧ ⑨ ⑩
INTERRUPTING OTHERS	① ② ③ ④ ⑤ ⑥ ⑦ ⑧ ⑨ ⑩
EASILY FRUSTRATED	① ② ③ ④ ⑤ ⑥ ⑦ ⑧ ⑨ ⑩
UNABLE TO HOLD BACK EMOTIONS	① ② ③ ④ ⑤ ⑥ ⑦ ⑧ ⑨ ⑩

MEALS	MEDICATIONS

Water Tracker

NOTES

....
....

Mood Tracker

BEHAVIOR

INATTENTION

SHORT ATTENTION	① ② ③ ④ ⑤ ⑥ ⑦ ⑧ ⑨ ⑩
UNMOTIVATED / BORED	① ② ③ ④ ⑤ ⑥ ⑦ ⑧ ⑨ ⑩
SHORT ATTENTION	① ② ③ ④ ⑤ ⑥ ⑦ ⑧ ⑨ ⑩
FORGETFUL / CONFUSIONED	① ② ③ ④ ⑤ ⑥ ⑦ ⑧ ⑨ ⑩

HYPERACTIVITY

CONSTANTLY MOVING / TALKING	① ② ③ ④ ⑤ ⑥ ⑦ ⑧ ⑨ ⑩
STRUGGLING TO SIT STILL	① ② ③ ④ ⑤ ⑥ ⑦ ⑧ ⑨ ⑩
TOUCHING THINGS REPEATEDLY	① ② ③ ④ ⑤ ⑥ ⑦ ⑧ ⑨ ⑩
DIFFICULT SLEEPING	① ② ③ ④ ⑤ ⑥ ⑦ ⑧ ⑨ ⑩

IMPULSIVITY

ACTING WITHOUT THINKING	① ② ③ ④ ⑤ ⑥ ⑦ ⑧ ⑨ ⑩
INTERRUPTING OTHERS	① ② ③ ④ ⑤ ⑥ ⑦ ⑧ ⑨ ⑩
EASILY FRUSTRATED	① ② ③ ④ ⑤ ⑥ ⑦ ⑧ ⑨ ⑩
UNABLE TO HOLD BACK EMOTIONS	① ② ③ ④ ⑤ ⑥ ⑦ ⑧ ⑨ ⑩

MEALS

MEDICATIONS

Water Tracker

NOTES

Mood Tracker

BEHAVIOR

INATTENTION

SHORT ATTENTION	① ② ③ ④ ⑤ ⑥ ⑦ ⑧ ⑨ ⑩
UNMOTIVATED / BORED	① ② ③ ④ ⑤ ⑥ ⑦ ⑧ ⑨ ⑩
SHORT ATTENTION	① ② ③ ④ ⑤ ⑥ ⑦ ⑧ ⑨ ⑩
FORGETFUL / CONFUSIONED	① ② ③ ④ ⑤ ⑥ ⑦ ⑧ ⑨ ⑩

HYPERACTIVITY

CONSTANTLY MOVING / TALKING	① ② ③ ④ ⑤ ⑥ ⑦ ⑧ ⑨ ⑩
STRUGGLING TO SIT STILL	① ② ③ ④ ⑤ ⑥ ⑦ ⑧ ⑨ ⑩
TOUCHING THINGS REPEATEDLY	① ② ③ ④ ⑤ ⑥ ⑦ ⑧ ⑨ ⑩
DIFFICULT SLEEPING	① ② ③ ④ ⑤ ⑥ ⑦ ⑧ ⑨ ⑩

IMPULSIVITY

ACTING WITHOUT THINKING	① ② ③ ④ ⑤ ⑥ ⑦ ⑧ ⑨ ⑩
INTERRUPTING OTHERS	① ② ③ ④ ⑤ ⑥ ⑦ ⑧ ⑨ ⑩
EASILY FRUSTRATED	① ② ③ ④ ⑤ ⑥ ⑦ ⑧ ⑨ ⑩
UNABLE TO HOLD BACK EMOTIONS	① ② ③ ④ ⑤ ⑥ ⑦ ⑧ ⑨ ⑩

MEALS

MEDICATIONS

Water Tracker

NOTES

Mood Tracker

INATTENTION

SHORT ATTENTION	1 2 3 4 5 6 7 8 9 10
UNMOTIVATED / BORED	1 2 3 4 5 6 7 8 9 10
SHORT ATTENTION	1 2 3 4 5 6 7 8 9 10
FORGETFUL / CONFUSIONED	1 2 3 4 5 6 7 8 9 10

HYPERACTIVITY

CONSTANTLY MOVING / TALKING	1 2 3 4 5 6 7 8 9 10
STRUGGLING TO SIT STILL	1 2 3 4 5 6 7 8 9 10
TOUCHING THINGS REPEATEDLY	1 2 3 4 5 6 7 8 9 10
DIFFICULT SLEEPING	1 2 3 4 5 6 7 8 9 10

IMPULSIVITY

ACTING WITHOUT THINKING	1 2 3 4 5 6 7 8 9 10
INTERRUPTING OTHERS	1 2 3 4 5 6 7 8 9 10
EASILY FRUSTRATED	1 2 3 4 5 6 7 8 9 10
UNABLE TO HOLD BACK EMOTIONS	1 2 3 4 5 6 7 8 9 10

MEALS

MEDICATIONS

Water Tracker

NOTES

<table><tr><td>

DAY GOALS

1 ....
2 ....
3 ....

</td><td>

DATE

WEEK

LOCATION

WEIGHT

</td></tr></table>

Mood Tracker

BEHAVIOR

INATTENTION

SHORT ATTENTION	① ② ③ ④ ⑤ ⑥ ⑦ ⑧ ⑨ ⑩
UNMOTIVATED / BORED	① ② ③ ④ ⑤ ⑥ ⑦ ⑧ ⑨ ⑩
SHORT ATTENTION	① ② ③ ④ ⑤ ⑥ ⑦ ⑧ ⑨ ⑩
FORGETFUL / CONFUSIONED	① ② ③ ④ ⑤ ⑥ ⑦ ⑧ ⑨ ⑩

HYPERACTIVITY

CONSTANTLY MOVING / TALKING	① ② ③ ④ ⑤ ⑥ ⑦ ⑧ ⑨ ⑩
STRUGGLING TO SIT STILL	① ② ③ ④ ⑤ ⑥ ⑦ ⑧ ⑨ ⑩
TOUCHING THINGS REPEATEDLY	① ② ③ ④ ⑤ ⑥ ⑦ ⑧ ⑨ ⑩
DIFFICULT SLEEPING	① ② ③ ④ ⑤ ⑥ ⑦ ⑧ ⑨ ⑩

IMPULSIVITY

ACTING WITHOUT THINKING	① ② ③ ④ ⑤ ⑥ ⑦ ⑧ ⑨ ⑩
INTERRUPTING OTHERS	① ② ③ ④ ⑤ ⑥ ⑦ ⑧ ⑨ ⑩
EASILY FRUSTRATED	① ② ③ ④ ⑤ ⑥ ⑦ ⑧ ⑨ ⑩
UNABLE TO HOLD BACK EMOTIONS	① ② ③ ④ ⑤ ⑥ ⑦ ⑧ ⑨ ⑩

MEALS	MEDICATIONS

Water Tracker

NOTES

....
....

Mood Tracker

BEHAVIOR

INATTENTION

SHORT ATTENTION	1 2 3 4 5 6 7 8 9 10
UNMOTIVATED / BORED	1 2 3 4 5 6 7 8 9 10
SHORT ATTENTION	1 2 3 4 5 6 7 8 9 10
FORGETFUL / CONFUSIONED	1 2 3 4 5 6 7 8 9 10

HYPERACTIVITY

CONSTANTLY MOVING / TALKING	1 2 3 4 5 6 7 8 9 10
STRUGGLING TO SIT STILL	1 2 3 4 5 6 7 8 9 10
TOUCHING THINGS REPEATEDLY	1 2 3 4 5 6 7 8 9 10
DIFFICULT SLEEPING	1 2 3 4 5 6 7 8 9 10

IMPULSIVITY

ACTING WITHOUT THINKING	1 2 3 4 5 6 7 8 9 10
INTERRUPTING OTHERS	1 2 3 4 5 6 7 8 9 10
EASILY FRUSTRATED	1 2 3 4 5 6 7 8 9 10
UNABLE TO HOLD BACK EMOTIONS	1 2 3 4 5 6 7 8 9 10

MEALS

MEDICATIONS

Water Tracker

NOTES

DAY GOALS

1 ....
2 ....
3 ....

DATE

WEEK

LOCATION

WEIGHT

Mood Tracker

BEHAVIOR

INATTENTION

SHORT ATTENTION	① ② ③ ④ ⑤ ⑥ ⑦ ⑧ ⑨ ⑩
UNMOTIVATED / BORED	① ② ③ ④ ⑤ ⑥ ⑦ ⑧ ⑨ ⑩
SHORT ATTENTION	① ② ③ ④ ⑤ ⑥ ⑦ ⑧ ⑨ ⑩
FORGETFUL / CONFUSIONED	① ② ③ ④ ⑤ ⑥ ⑦ ⑧ ⑨ ⑩

HYPERACTIVITY

CONSTANTLY MOVING / TALKING	① ② ③ ④ ⑤ ⑥ ⑦ ⑧ ⑨ ⑩
STRUGGLING TO SIT STILL	① ② ③ ④ ⑤ ⑥ ⑦ ⑧ ⑨ ⑩
TOUCHING THINGS REPEATEDLY	① ② ③ ④ ⑤ ⑥ ⑦ ⑧ ⑨ ⑩
DIFFICULT SLEEPING	① ② ③ ④ ⑤ ⑥ ⑦ ⑧ ⑨ ⑩

IMPULSIVITY

ACTING WITHOUT THINKING	① ② ③ ④ ⑤ ⑥ ⑦ ⑧ ⑨ ⑩
INTERRUPTING OTHERS	① ② ③ ④ ⑤ ⑥ ⑦ ⑧ ⑨ ⑩
EASILY FRUSTRATED	① ② ③ ④ ⑤ ⑥ ⑦ ⑧ ⑨ ⑩
UNABLE TO HOLD BACK EMOTIONS	① ② ③ ④ ⑤ ⑥ ⑦ ⑧ ⑨ ⑩

MEALS

MEDICATIONS

Water Tracker

NOTES

....
....

<table>
<tr><td>

DAY GOALS

1 ....
2 ....
3 ....

</td><td>

DATE

WEEK

LOCATION

WEIGHT

</td></tr>
</table>

Mood Tracker

BEHAVIOR

INATTENTION

SHORT ATTENTION	① ② ③ ④ ⑤ ⑥ ⑦ ⑧ ⑨ ⑩
UNMOTIVATED / BORED	① ② ③ ④ ⑤ ⑥ ⑦ ⑧ ⑨ ⑩
SHORT ATTENTION	① ② ③ ④ ⑤ ⑥ ⑦ ⑧ ⑨ ⑩
FORGETFUL / CONFUSIONED	① ② ③ ④ ⑤ ⑥ ⑦ ⑧ ⑨ ⑩

HYPERACTIVITY

CONSTANTLY MOVING / TALKING	① ② ③ ④ ⑤ ⑥ ⑦ ⑧ ⑨ ⑩
STRUGGLING TO SIT STILL	① ② ③ ④ ⑤ ⑥ ⑦ ⑧ ⑨ ⑩
TOUCHING THINGS REPEATEDLY	① ② ③ ④ ⑤ ⑥ ⑦ ⑧ ⑨ ⑩
DIFFICULT SLEEPING	① ② ③ ④ ⑤ ⑥ ⑦ ⑧ ⑨ ⑩

IMPULSIVITY

ACTING WITHOUT THINKING	① ② ③ ④ ⑤ ⑥ ⑦ ⑧ ⑨ ⑩
INTERRUPTING OTHERS	① ② ③ ④ ⑤ ⑥ ⑦ ⑧ ⑨ ⑩
EASILY FRUSTRATED	① ② ③ ④ ⑤ ⑥ ⑦ ⑧ ⑨ ⑩
UNABLE TO HOLD BACK EMOTIONS	① ② ③ ④ ⑤ ⑥ ⑦ ⑧ ⑨ ⑩

MEALS

MEDICATIONS

Water Tracker

NOTES

....
....

Mood Tracker

BEHAVIOR

INATTENTION

SHORT ATTENTION	1 2 3 4 5 6 7 8 9 10
UNMOTIVATED / BORED	1 2 3 4 5 6 7 8 9 10
SHORT ATTENTION	1 2 3 4 5 6 7 8 9 10
FORGETFUL / CONFUSIONED	1 2 3 4 5 6 7 8 9 10

HYPERACTIVITY

CONSTANTLY MOVING / TALKING	1 2 3 4 5 6 7 8 9 10
STRUGGLING TO SIT STILL	1 2 3 4 5 6 7 8 9 10
TOUCHING THINGS REPEATEDLY	1 2 3 4 5 6 7 8 9 10
DIFFICULT SLEEPING	1 2 3 4 5 6 7 8 9 10

IMPULSIVITY

ACTING WITHOUT THINKING	1 2 3 4 5 6 7 8 9 10
INTERRUPTING OTHERS	1 2 3 4 5 6 7 8 9 10
EASILY FRUSTRATED	1 2 3 4 5 6 7 8 9 10
UNABLE TO HOLD BACK EMOTIONS	1 2 3 4 5 6 7 8 9 10

MEALS

MEDICATIONS

Water Tracker

NOTES

<table>
<tr><td>

DAY GOALS

1 ....
2 ....
3 ....

</td><td>

DATE

WEEK

LOCATION

WEIGHT

</td></tr>
</table>

Mood Tracker

BEHAVIOR

INATTENTION

SHORT ATTENTION	① ② ③ ④ ⑤ ⑥ ⑦ ⑧ ⑨ ⑩
UNMOTIVATED / BORED	① ② ③ ④ ⑤ ⑥ ⑦ ⑧ ⑨ ⑩
SHORT ATTENTION	① ② ③ ④ ⑤ ⑥ ⑦ ⑧ ⑨ ⑩
FORGETFUL / CONFUSIONED	① ② ③ ④ ⑤ ⑥ ⑦ ⑧ ⑨ ⑩

HYPERACTIVITY

CONSTANTLY MOVING / TALKING	① ② ③ ④ ⑤ ⑥ ⑦ ⑧ ⑨ ⑩
STRUGGLING TO SIT STILL	① ② ③ ④ ⑤ ⑥ ⑦ ⑧ ⑨ ⑩
TOUCHING THINGS REPEATEDLY	① ② ③ ④ ⑤ ⑥ ⑦ ⑧ ⑨ ⑩
DIFFICULT SLEEPING	① ② ③ ④ ⑤ ⑥ ⑦ ⑧ ⑨ ⑩

IMPULSIVITY

ACTING WITHOUT THINKING	① ② ③ ④ ⑤ ⑥ ⑦ ⑧ ⑨ ⑩
INTERRUPTING OTHERS	① ② ③ ④ ⑤ ⑥ ⑦ ⑧ ⑨ ⑩
EASILY FRUSTRATED	① ② ③ ④ ⑤ ⑥ ⑦ ⑧ ⑨ ⑩
UNABLE TO HOLD BACK EMOTIONS	① ② ③ ④ ⑤ ⑥ ⑦ ⑧ ⑨ ⑩

MEALS	MEDICATIONS

Water Tracker

NOTES

....
....

<table>
<tr><td>

DAY GOALS

1 ....
2 ....
3 ....

</td><td>

DATE

WEEK

LOCATION

WEIGHT

</td></tr>
</table>

Mood Tracker

BEHAVIOR

INATTENTION

SHORT ATTENTION	① ② ③ ④ ⑤ ⑥ ⑦ ⑧ ⑨ ⑩
UNMOTIVATED / BORED	① ② ③ ④ ⑤ ⑥ ⑦ ⑧ ⑨ ⑩
SHORT ATTENTION	① ② ③ ④ ⑤ ⑥ ⑦ ⑧ ⑨ ⑩
FORGETFUL / CONFUSIONED	① ② ③ ④ ⑤ ⑥ ⑦ ⑧ ⑨ ⑩

HYPERACTIVITY

CONSTANTLY MOVING / TALKING	① ② ③ ④ ⑤ ⑥ ⑦ ⑧ ⑨ ⑩
STRUGGLING TO SIT STILL	① ② ③ ④ ⑤ ⑥ ⑦ ⑧ ⑨ ⑩
TOUCHING THINGS REPEATEDLY	① ② ③ ④ ⑤ ⑥ ⑦ ⑧ ⑨ ⑩
DIFFICULT SLEEPING	① ② ③ ④ ⑤ ⑥ ⑦ ⑧ ⑨ ⑩

IMPULSIVITY

ACTING WITHOUT THINKING	① ② ③ ④ ⑤ ⑥ ⑦ ⑧ ⑨ ⑩
INTERRUPTING OTHERS	① ② ③ ④ ⑤ ⑥ ⑦ ⑧ ⑨ ⑩
EASILY FRUSTRATED	① ② ③ ④ ⑤ ⑥ ⑦ ⑧ ⑨ ⑩
UNABLE TO HOLD BACK EMOTIONS	① ② ③ ④ ⑤ ⑥ ⑦ ⑧ ⑨ ⑩

MEALS	MEDICATIONS

Water Tracker

NOTES

....

....

<table>
<tr><td>

DAY GOALS

1 ....
2 ....
3 ....

</td><td>

DATE

WEEK

LOCATION

WEIGHT

</td></tr>
</table>

Mood Tracker ☹ 😐 😣 😢 😠 😀

BEHAVIOR

INATTENTION

SHORT ATTENTION	① ② ③ ④ ⑤ ⑥ ⑦ ⑧ ⑨ ⑩
UNMOTIVATED / BORED	① ② ③ ④ ⑤ ⑥ ⑦ ⑧ ⑨ ⑩
SHORT ATTENTION	① ② ③ ④ ⑤ ⑥ ⑦ ⑧ ⑨ ⑩
FORGETFUL / CONFUSIONED	① ② ③ ④ ⑤ ⑥ ⑦ ⑧ ⑨ ⑩

HYPERACTIVITY

CONSTANTLY MOVING / TALKING	① ② ③ ④ ⑤ ⑥ ⑦ ⑧ ⑨ ⑩
STRUGGLING TO SIT STILL	① ② ③ ④ ⑤ ⑥ ⑦ ⑧ ⑨ ⑩
TOUCHING THINGS REPEATEDLY	① ② ③ ④ ⑤ ⑥ ⑦ ⑧ ⑨ ⑩
DIFFICULT SLEEPING	① ② ③ ④ ⑤ ⑥ ⑦ ⑧ ⑨ ⑩

IMPULSIVITY

ACTING WITHOUT THINKING	① ② ③ ④ ⑤ ⑥ ⑦ ⑧ ⑨ ⑩
INTERRUPTING OTHERS	① ② ③ ④ ⑤ ⑥ ⑦ ⑧ ⑨ ⑩
EASILY FRUSTRATED	① ② ③ ④ ⑤ ⑥ ⑦ ⑧ ⑨ ⑩
UNABLE TO HOLD BACK EMOTIONS	① ② ③ ④ ⑤ ⑥ ⑦ ⑧ ⑨ ⑩

MEALS

MEDICATIONS

Water Tracker

NOTES

....
....

<table>
<tr><td>

DAY GOALS

1 ....
2 ....
3 ....

</td><td>

DATE

WEEK

LOCATION

WEIGHT

</td></tr>
</table>

Mood Tracker

BEHAVIOR

INATTENTION

SHORT ATTENTION	① ② ③ ④ ⑤ ⑥ ⑦ ⑧ ⑨ ⑩
UNMOTIVATED / BORED	① ② ③ ④ ⑤ ⑥ ⑦ ⑧ ⑨ ⑩
SHORT ATTENTION	① ② ③ ④ ⑤ ⑥ ⑦ ⑧ ⑨ ⑩
FORGETFUL / CONFUSIONED	① ② ③ ④ ⑤ ⑥ ⑦ ⑧ ⑨ ⑩

HYPERACTIVITY

CONSTANTLY MOVING / TALKING	① ② ③ ④ ⑤ ⑥ ⑦ ⑧ ⑨ ⑩
STRUGGLING TO SIT STILL	① ② ③ ④ ⑤ ⑥ ⑦ ⑧ ⑨ ⑩
TOUCHING THINGS REPEATEDLY	① ② ③ ④ ⑤ ⑥ ⑦ ⑧ ⑨ ⑩
DIFFICULT SLEEPING	① ② ③ ④ ⑤ ⑥ ⑦ ⑧ ⑨ ⑩

IMPULSIVITY

ACTING WITHOUT THINKING	① ② ③ ④ ⑤ ⑥ ⑦ ⑧ ⑨ ⑩
INTERRUPTING OTHERS	① ② ③ ④ ⑤ ⑥ ⑦ ⑧ ⑨ ⑩
EASILY FRUSTRATED	① ② ③ ④ ⑤ ⑥ ⑦ ⑧ ⑨ ⑩
UNABLE TO HOLD BACK EMOTIONS	① ② ③ ④ ⑤ ⑥ ⑦ ⑧ ⑨ ⑩

MEALS

MEDICATIONS

Water Tracker

NOTES

....
....

<table>
<tr><td>

DAY GOALS

1 ....

2 ....

3 ....

</td><td>

DATE

WEEK

LOCATION

WEIGHT

</td></tr>
</table>

Mood Tracker

BEHAVIOR

INATTENTION

SHORT ATTENTION	① ② ③ ④ ⑤ ⑥ ⑦ ⑧ ⑨ ⑩
UNMOTIVATED / BORED	① ② ③ ④ ⑤ ⑥ ⑦ ⑧ ⑨ ⑩
SHORT ATTENTION	① ② ③ ④ ⑤ ⑥ ⑦ ⑧ ⑨ ⑩
FORGETFUL / CONFUSIONED	① ② ③ ④ ⑤ ⑥ ⑦ ⑧ ⑨ ⑩

HYPERACTIVITY

CONSTANTLY MOVING / TALKING	① ② ③ ④ ⑤ ⑥ ⑦ ⑧ ⑨ ⑩
STRUGGLING TO SIT STILL	① ② ③ ④ ⑤ ⑥ ⑦ ⑧ ⑨ ⑩
TOUCHING THINGS REPEATEDLY	① ② ③ ④ ⑤ ⑥ ⑦ ⑧ ⑨ ⑩
DIFFICULT SLEEPING	① ② ③ ④ ⑤ ⑥ ⑦ ⑧ ⑨ ⑩

IMPULSIVITY

ACTING WITHOUT THINKING	① ② ③ ④ ⑤ ⑥ ⑦ ⑧ ⑨ ⑩
INTERRUPTING OTHERS	① ② ③ ④ ⑤ ⑥ ⑦ ⑧ ⑨ ⑩
EASILY FRUSTRATED	① ② ③ ④ ⑤ ⑥ ⑦ ⑧ ⑨ ⑩
UNABLE TO HOLD BACK EMOTIONS	① ② ③ ④ ⑤ ⑥ ⑦ ⑧ ⑨ ⑩

MEALS

MEDICATIONS

Water Tracker

NOTES

....

....

<table>
<tr><td>DAY GOALS</td><td>DATE</td></tr>
<tr><td>1 ....
2 ....
3 ....</td><td>WEEK
LOCATION
WEIGHT</td></tr>
</table>

Mood Tracker

BEHAVIOR

INATTENTION

SHORT ATTENTION	① ② ③ ④ ⑤ ⑥ ⑦ ⑧ ⑨ ⑩
UNMOTIVATED / BORED	① ② ③ ④ ⑤ ⑥ ⑦ ⑧ ⑨ ⑩
SHORT ATTENTION	① ② ③ ④ ⑤ ⑥ ⑦ ⑧ ⑨ ⑩
FORGETFUL / CONFUSIONED	① ② ③ ④ ⑤ ⑥ ⑦ ⑧ ⑨ ⑩

HYPERACTIVITY

CONSTANTLY MOVING / TALKING	① ② ③ ④ ⑤ ⑥ ⑦ ⑧ ⑨ ⑩
STRUGGLING TO SIT STILL	① ② ③ ④ ⑤ ⑥ ⑦ ⑧ ⑨ ⑩
TOUCHING THINGS REPEATEDLY	① ② ③ ④ ⑤ ⑥ ⑦ ⑧ ⑨ ⑩
DIFFICULT SLEEPING	① ② ③ ④ ⑤ ⑥ ⑦ ⑧ ⑨ ⑩

IMPULSIVITY

ACTING WITHOUT THINKING	① ② ③ ④ ⑤ ⑥ ⑦ ⑧ ⑨ ⑩
INTERRUPTING OTHERS	① ② ③ ④ ⑤ ⑥ ⑦ ⑧ ⑨ ⑩
EASILY FRUSTRATED	① ② ③ ④ ⑤ ⑥ ⑦ ⑧ ⑨ ⑩
UNABLE TO HOLD BACK EMOTIONS	① ② ③ ④ ⑤ ⑥ ⑦ ⑧ ⑨ ⑩

MEALS

MEDICATIONS

Water Tracker

NOTES

....
....

<table>
<tr><td>

DAY GOALS

1 ....
2 ....
3 ....

</td><td>

DATE

WEEK

LOCATION

WEIGHT

</td></tr>
</table>

Mood Tracker

BEHAVIOR

INATTENTION

SHORT ATTENTION	① ② ③ ④ ⑤ ⑥ ⑦ ⑧ ⑨ ⑩
UNMOTIVATED / BORED	① ② ③ ④ ⑤ ⑥ ⑦ ⑧ ⑨ ⑩
SHORT ATTENTION	① ② ③ ④ ⑤ ⑥ ⑦ ⑧ ⑨ ⑩
FORGETFUL / CONFUSIONED	① ② ③ ④ ⑤ ⑥ ⑦ ⑧ ⑨ ⑩

HYPERACTIVITY

CONSTANTLY MOVING / TALKING	① ② ③ ④ ⑤ ⑥ ⑦ ⑧ ⑨ ⑩
STRUGGLING TO SIT STILL	① ② ③ ④ ⑤ ⑥ ⑦ ⑧ ⑨ ⑩
TOUCHING THINGS REPEATEDLY	① ② ③ ④ ⑤ ⑥ ⑦ ⑧ ⑨ ⑩
DIFFICULT SLEEPING	① ② ③ ④ ⑤ ⑥ ⑦ ⑧ ⑨ ⑩

IMPULSIVITY

ACTING WITHOUT THINKING	① ② ③ ④ ⑤ ⑥ ⑦ ⑧ ⑨ ⑩
INTERRUPTING OTHERS	① ② ③ ④ ⑤ ⑥ ⑦ ⑧ ⑨ ⑩
EASILY FRUSTRATED	① ② ③ ④ ⑤ ⑥ ⑦ ⑧ ⑨ ⑩
UNABLE TO HOLD BACK EMOTIONS	① ② ③ ④ ⑤ ⑥ ⑦ ⑧ ⑨ ⑩

MEALS	MEDICATIONS

Water Tracker

NOTES

....
....

1 ....
2 ....
3 ....

DATE

WEEK

LOCATION

WEIGHT

Mood Tracker

BEHAVIOR

INATTENTION

SHORT ATTENTION ① ② ③ ④ ⑤ ⑥ ⑦ ⑧ ⑨ ⑩

UNMOTIVATED / BORED ① ② ③ ④ ⑤ ⑥ ⑦ ⑧ ⑨ ⑩

SHORT ATTENTION ① ② ③ ④ ⑤ ⑥ ⑦ ⑧ ⑨ ⑩

FORGETFUL / CONFUSIONED ① ② ③ ④ ⑤ ⑥ ⑦ ⑧ ⑨ ⑩

HYPERACTIVITY

CONSTANTLY MOVING / TALKING ① ② ③ ④ ⑤ ⑥ ⑦ ⑧ ⑨ ⑩

STRUGGLING TO SIT STILL ① ② ③ ④ ⑤ ⑥ ⑦ ⑧ ⑨ ⑩

TOUCHING THINGS REPEATEDLY ① ② ③ ④ ⑤ ⑥ ⑦ ⑧ ⑨ ⑩

DIFFICULT SLEEPING ① ② ③ ④ ⑤ ⑥ ⑦ ⑧ ⑨ ⑩

IMPULSIVITY

ACTING WITHOUT THINKING ① ② ③ ④ ⑤ ⑥ ⑦ ⑧ ⑨ ⑩

INTERRUPTING OTHERS ① ② ③ ④ ⑤ ⑥ ⑦ ⑧ ⑨ ⑩

EASILY FRUSTRATED ① ② ③ ④ ⑤ ⑥ ⑦ ⑧ ⑨ ⑩

UNABLE TO HOLD BACK EMOTIONS ① ② ③ ④ ⑤ ⑥ ⑦ ⑧ ⑨ ⑩

MEALS

MEDICATIONS

Water Tracker

NOTES

....

....

<table>
<tr><td>

DAY GOALS

1 ....

2 ....

3 ....

</td><td>

DATE

WEEK

LOCATION

WEIGHT

</td></tr>
</table>

Mood Tracker

BEHAVIOR

INATTENTION

SHORT ATTENTION	① ② ③ ④ ⑤ ⑥ ⑦ ⑧ ⑨ ⑩
UNMOTIVATED / BORED	① ② ③ ④ ⑤ ⑥ ⑦ ⑧ ⑨ ⑩
SHORT ATTENTION	① ② ③ ④ ⑤ ⑥ ⑦ ⑧ ⑨ ⑩
FORGETFUL / CONFUSIONED	① ② ③ ④ ⑤ ⑥ ⑦ ⑧ ⑨ ⑩

HYPERACTIVITY

CONSTANTLY MOVING / TALKING	① ② ③ ④ ⑤ ⑥ ⑦ ⑧ ⑨ ⑩
STRUGGLING TO SIT STILL	① ② ③ ④ ⑤ ⑥ ⑦ ⑧ ⑨ ⑩
TOUCHING THINGS REPEATEDLY	① ② ③ ④ ⑤ ⑥ ⑦ ⑧ ⑨ ⑩
DIFFICULT SLEEPING	① ② ③ ④ ⑤ ⑥ ⑦ ⑧ ⑨ ⑩

IMPULSIVITY

ACTING WITHOUT THINKING	① ② ③ ④ ⑤ ⑥ ⑦ ⑧ ⑨ ⑩
INTERRUPTING OTHERS	① ② ③ ④ ⑤ ⑥ ⑦ ⑧ ⑨ ⑩
EASILY FRUSTRATED	① ② ③ ④ ⑤ ⑥ ⑦ ⑧ ⑨ ⑩
UNABLE TO HOLD BACK EMOTIONS	① ② ③ ④ ⑤ ⑥ ⑦ ⑧ ⑨ ⑩

MEALS	MEDICATIONS

Water Tracker

NOTES

....

....

<table>
<tr><td>

DAY GOALS

1 ....
2 ....
3 ....

</td><td>

DATE

WEEK

LOCATION

WEIGHT

</td></tr>
</table>

Mood Tracker

BEHAVIOR

INATTENTION

SHORT ATTENTION   ① ② ③ ④ ⑤ ⑥ ⑦ ⑧ ⑨ ⑩

UNMOTIVATED / BORED   ① ② ③ ④ ⑤ ⑥ ⑦ ⑧ ⑨ ⑩

SHORT ATTENTION   ① ② ③ ④ ⑤ ⑥ ⑦ ⑧ ⑨ ⑩

FORGETFUL / CONFUSIONED   ① ② ③ ④ ⑤ ⑥ ⑦ ⑧ ⑨ ⑩

HYPERACTIVITY

CONSTANTLY MOVING / TALKING   ① ② ③ ④ ⑤ ⑥ ⑦ ⑧ ⑨ ⑩

STRUGGLING TO SIT STILL   ① ② ③ ④ ⑤ ⑥ ⑦ ⑧ ⑨ ⑩

TOUCHING THINGS REPEATEDLY   ① ② ③ ④ ⑤ ⑥ ⑦ ⑧ ⑨ ⑩

DIFFICULT SLEEPING   ① ② ③ ④ ⑤ ⑥ ⑦ ⑧ ⑨ ⑩

IMPULSIVITY

ACTING WITHOUT THINKING   ① ② ③ ④ ⑤ ⑥ ⑦ ⑧ ⑨ ⑩

INTERRUPTING OTHERS   ① ② ③ ④ ⑤ ⑥ ⑦ ⑧ ⑨ ⑩

EASILY FRUSTRATED   ① ② ③ ④ ⑤ ⑥ ⑦ ⑧ ⑨ ⑩

UNABLE TO HOLD BACK EMOTIONS   ① ② ③ ④ ⑤ ⑥ ⑦ ⑧ ⑨ ⑩

MEALS

MEDICATIONS

Water Tracker

NOTES

....
....

<table><tr><td>

DAY GOALS

1 ....
2 ....
3 ....

</td><td>

DATE

WEEK

LOCATION

WEIGHT

</td></tr></table>

Mood Tracker

BEHAVIOR

INATTENTION

SHORT ATTENTION	① ② ③ ④ ⑤ ⑥ ⑦ ⑧ ⑨ ⑩
UNMOTIVATED / BORED	① ② ③ ④ ⑤ ⑥ ⑦ ⑧ ⑨ ⑩
SHORT ATTENTION	① ② ③ ④ ⑤ ⑥ ⑦ ⑧ ⑨ ⑩
FORGETFUL / CONFUSIONED	① ② ③ ④ ⑤ ⑥ ⑦ ⑧ ⑨ ⑩

HYPERACTIVITY

CONSTANTLY MOVING / TALKING	① ② ③ ④ ⑤ ⑥ ⑦ ⑧ ⑨ ⑩
STRUGGLING TO SIT STILL	① ② ③ ④ ⑤ ⑥ ⑦ ⑧ ⑨ ⑩
TOUCHING THINGS REPEATEDLY	① ② ③ ④ ⑤ ⑥ ⑦ ⑧ ⑨ ⑩
DIFFICULT SLEEPING	① ② ③ ④ ⑤ ⑥ ⑦ ⑧ ⑨ ⑩

IMPULSIVITY

ACTING WITHOUT THINKING	① ② ③ ④ ⑤ ⑥ ⑦ ⑧ ⑨ ⑩
INTERRUPTING OTHERS	① ② ③ ④ ⑤ ⑥ ⑦ ⑧ ⑨ ⑩
EASILY FRUSTRATED	① ② ③ ④ ⑤ ⑥ ⑦ ⑧ ⑨ ⑩
UNABLE TO HOLD BACK EMOTIONS	① ② ③ ④ ⑤ ⑥ ⑦ ⑧ ⑨ ⑩

MEALS

MEDICATIONS

Water Tracker

NOTES

....
....

Mood Tracker

BEHAVIOR

INATTENTION

SHORT ATTENTION	1 2 3 4 5 6 7 8 9 10
UNMOTIVATED / BORED	1 2 3 4 5 6 7 8 9 10
SHORT ATTENTION	1 2 3 4 5 6 7 8 9 10
FORGETFUL / CONFUSIONED	1 2 3 4 5 6 7 8 9 10

HYPERACTIVITY

CONSTANTLY MOVING / TALKING	1 2 3 4 5 6 7 8 9 10
STRUGGLING TO SIT STILL	1 2 3 4 5 6 7 8 9 10
TOUCHING THINGS REPEATEDLY	1 2 3 4 5 6 7 8 9 10
DIFFICULT SLEEPING	1 2 3 4 5 6 7 8 9 10

IMPULSIVITY

ACTING WITHOUT THINKING	1 2 3 4 5 6 7 8 9 10
INTERRUPTING OTHERS	1 2 3 4 5 6 7 8 9 10
EASILY FRUSTRATED	1 2 3 4 5 6 7 8 9 10
UNABLE TO HOLD BACK EMOTIONS	1 2 3 4 5 6 7 8 9 10

MEALS

MEDICATIONS

Water Tracker

NOTES